ISBN 978-0-483-51506-2
PIBN 10110941

This book is a reproduction of an important historical work. Forgotten Books uses
state-of-the-art technology to digitally reconstruct the work, preserving the original format
whilst repairing imperfections present in the aged copy. In rare cases, an imperfection in
the original, such as a blemish or missing page, may be replicated in our edition. We do,
however, repair the vast majority of imperfections successfully; any imperfections that
remain are intentionally left to preserve the state of such historical works.

TESTIMONIALS.

Most of the following Testimonials as to the attractiveness and real value of the accompanying work, were received by the Publishers before the printed sheets were placed in the hands of the binder :

From REV. J. E. GOODRICH, *Professor of Rhetoric and of English Literature.*

UNIVERSITY OF VERMONT, *March* 19*th,* 1874.

I have read the Rev. L. N. BEAUDRY's MS., "Spiritual Struggles of a Roman Catholic," with much interest—an intreste which increased as the narrative advanced. The work is well adapted not only to enlighten the Protestant as to the substance and methods of Romanism, but also to help him to appreciate the religious convictions and mental and moral strivings of his fellow-Christians of the Roman Catholic faith. To the Roman Catholic also, who may read it, it cannot but prove an easy and agreeable introduction to the simplicity and freedom of the Gospel, as taught in the Reformed Churche . The volume would be a desirable addition to the Sunday-school library. The structure of the work, consisting, as it does, of a series of conversations, seems to commend it specially to the persual of the young.

From REV. E. WENTWORTH, *Editor "Ladies Repository."*

The "Spiritual Struggles of a Roman Catholic," by the Rev. Louis N. Beaudry, of the Troy Conference, is just the thing I have been long looking for from Mr. Beaudry's pen. I have known him intimately in Conference relation for several years ; have heard portions, here and there, of his intensely interesting personal history, and have felt that he ought to write it out for the benefit of the world. This task he has at

a

ast accomplished in most fascinating style—a style that cannot fail to be attractive to readers of all classes. Coming, as his personal experience and revelations do, immediately at the heels of the Gladstone controversy in England, they cannot fail to shed floods of light upon the Roman question. His is no testimony fished up from the minds of the past, but we have before us a living witness to the peculiarities of Rome against which our fathers protested three centuries ago, against which old-world statesmen and governments are protesting with emphasis to-day, and against which it is the duty of every lover of freedom in thought, government, and religion, and every lover of his country, morality, and human progress, still to protest, till the "Man of Sin" be dethroned and destroyed.

From REV. JOSEPH COOK.

Your book dazzles me by the ingenuity of its plan. The narrative is developed with dramatic skill, and draws one on irresistibly. Even the argumentative portions appear to me likely to command attention from your younger, and they certainly will delight your older, readers. You will be sure to be read, and, I hope, translated. In French, German, and especially in Italian, this book would do good.

Next in merit to the plan is, in my opinion, the style. I do not mean to flatter when I say, I admire exceedingly its clearness, precision, ease, and grace.

From REV. JOSEPH E. KING, D.D.

Having been permitted to read from advanced sheets the "Spiritual Struggles of a Roman Catholic," by Rev. Louis N. Beaudry, I am prepared to say that this little volume should be in every Sunday-school in the entire Protestant Church.

Its plot is ingenious, its statement of facts and doctrine discreet and lucid, its argument free from extravagance and bigotry, its spirit admirably charitable : and the reader is drawn on from chapter to chapter with increasing fascination of interest to the end, and then regrets there is not another volume of it.

In the war of evangelical Christianity with papal corrup-

;ions, the press has as yet issued no such telling "hand-gre. 1ade" as this volume.

Put into the hands of a bewildered Catholic at that critical moment when he is mortified with the discovery that the morals of Protestants are superior to those of any Catholic of 1is acquaintance, it may be expected to work the miracle of 1isenchanting him of his blind bigotry. From that time we 1hall find him accessible to Gospel truth. I trust the book may be blessed to many thousands.

From REV. WASHINGTON FROTHINGHAM.

I have read this volume with intense interest. Its merits 1re rare and peculiar. It differs from everything in previous 1xistence. Protestants generally take an external view of Romanism. This is a revelation of its errors and dangers from the inside. No Romanist can refute its statements. The personal narrative is one of striking character. Its honesty of purpose is transparent. Its style is fresh. Its chief claim rests upon its absolute truth, and this it possesses to such a degree as to deserve a place among the best reading of the age.

From REV. JAMES M. KING, D.D., *Pastor of St. John's M. E. Church, New York City.*

I have read the advance sheets of the book published by Nelson & Phillips, entitled "Spiritual Struggles of a Roman Catholic." by Rev. L. N. Beaudry. I have been greatly interested and instructed. The book is written in a conversational style. It deals kindly with the deluded, and puts facts in such form as to lead by convincing the judgment. The writer has had such rare personal experience, and such cogent reasons for study, that his utterances have a right to be considered authoritative. It is a luxury to find a converted Romanist dealing with the deceived followers of Romanism with a charity that wins, instead of with a severity that repels. Good service will be done for Christianity if Mr. Beaudry's book shall have an extensive circulation.

From Rev. Martin E. Cady, A.M., Principal of Troy Conference Academy.

I have very carefully examined the proof-sheets of Rev, Louis N. Beaudry's new book, entitled "Spiritual Struggles." It is the experience of one struggling out of Romanism into Protestantism. The candour with which the author deals with Romanism will commend this volume to every truth-loving person.

The plan of the book is very happily conceived, presenting the narrative and the arguments, if they may be called such, in the form of familiar conversation. It is to be hoped that the book may have a wide circulation, especially in Roman Catholic communities, for it cannot fail of accomplishing a good work.

From Rev. C. H. Dunton, Prof. in Troy Conference Academy.

I cannot tell you how much I have enjoyed your last book, "Spiritual Struggles of a Roman Catholic." I read it from the first to the last page with a constantly deepening interest. Its circulation among our youth could not but prove a valuable service to Christianity.

From Rev. E. A. Whittier, Evangelist.

I have just completed the reading of "Spiritual Struggles of a Roman Catholic," and can most cheerfully commend the book to all.

The work progresses in interest as you advance from chapter to chapter, unfolding the numerous errors of Romanism in such a light, and with such a spirit, as cannot fail to commend it to all candid minds.

From Rev. William Butler, D.D.

The most candid, intelligent, and charitable *exposé* of the points involved in this controversy.

[Dr. Butler has chosen this book, out of the mass of literature on this subject, to be translated and published in Spanish, as a standard work for the permanent use of his missions in Mexico.—Editor.]

From TALMAGE'S "*Christian at Work.*"

The Rev. Louis N. Beaudry, a converted Romanist, and for many years "an intelligent, pious, and useful Christian minister," has produced in this work a fair, candid, and charitable exhibition of the peculiar errors through which Romanists are compelled to struggle in order to get into the light of Bible Christianity. We have read the work, expecting to find it disfigured by blotches of passion or deformed by spasms of anger, but are happy to say that it is entirely free from all language that can well give offence. Of course it opens the system of Romanism so that all may see it as it is, in its organized and articulated forces, as they act upon the minds of their victims. It has been so well coutrived as a system, the mightiest ever made, for the enslavement of the human intellect, that it is indeed hard to escape when once within its toils. Mr. Beaudry, in a simple, animated, and charming style, full of French vivacity and yet most earnest in purpose, has given us a narrative of hardships, struggles, and difficulties through which he passed to the peace of a well-assured hope. The work is written in a conversational manner, as though it had been spoken to friends eager to learn the story of its author's life. *We do not remember to have seen a volume better fitted than this for universal circulation among Protestants and Romanists.* There are very many Romanists dissatisfied with the religion they have inherited, yet they do not like to cast it off until they see what they can get in exchange. A kind, temperate, truthful little work like this would be of great service to such, provided they are able to read it. Then, too, Protestants may learn from these pages what are some of the serious difficulties with which conscientious Romanists must contend in any efforts they make toward personal emancipation.

From "*The Methodist Quarterly Review.*"

This is one of the many books bearing on the Romish question, and, in not a few respects, is one of the best. It is the work of a convert from Romanism, and in its tracing of the great transition is a true autobiography. The author was born in Vermont, but his parents were French Canadians, devotedly attached to the Roman Catholic Church, and diligent in inculcating its principles and practices upon their numerous children. He was convinced of the errors of Rome, and converted to the true Catholic faith, when about twenty years of age. The author's early training gives him a knowledge of the machinery of the Papal Church, its forms and ceremonies, its methods of argument and popular appeal. Moreover, he understands the superstitions and the prejudices, the thousand ties, strong, and yet by outside observers dimly seen, which bind to the hopes, the fears, and the beliefs of childhood and youth, and resist the introduction of clearer light. The story is given in the form of Sunday afternoon conversations with the author's children, and an occasional visitor. There is interwoven throughout a considerable amount of information in regard to Rome and its errors, and yet there is no bitterness, nor spirit of strife. The style is animated; and by the introduction of various characters, each thinking and talking from his or her own standpoint, the conversation becomes life-like and real, and the reader learns without the labour of acquisition. It is a book for our Sabbath-schools and young people generally.

From " The N. Y. Christian Advocate."

Here is a book that quietly answers a thousand questions that Protestants are continually asking with respect to the Romish system and practice, and with a full admission of all the excellent things that Romanism holds in common with the universal Church. Mr. Beaudry was once a Roman Catholic, honest and sincere, and is now a useful and beloved minister in the Troy Conference. In pleasant Sunday afternoon conversations in his own family he tells the story of his life, in response to an inquiry of his daughter, bringing out not only his own personal experience, with its successive steps and the influence that led to his conversion, but the grounds of the faith and usages that he abandoned. Events have turned public attention to Romanism in some of its aspects of public danger, and this little book is calculated to show it as a soul-ensnaring system. It ought to be widely read. Its spirit is one of Christian tenderness, and its style so simple and easy that old and young will find it pleasant to read.

From "The New Orleans Christian Advocate."

This work is better for its purpose than a learned and ela borate treatment in a theological way. It has the freshness of actual experience, and the fascination of a story, while it embraces the most salient points of the controversy with Papal error and superstition. Our Protestant readers will find it a book full of interest and instruction, and it will be found an excellent work to put into the hands of persons leaning to Roman Catholicism who are willing to read and be informed.

From "Zion's Herald," (Boston, Mass.)

In a story form, with much literary grace, rather than in the monotonous record of chronological incidents, the writer presents his early doubts, difficulties, reasonings, conflicts, and triumphs, as he emerged from the bonds of a superstitious formalism into light, trust, and peace of the Gospel. It is an excellent volume to circulate, and should be translated into the modern European languages. It will be an eloquent, although silent, evangelist.

From "The Rutland (Vt.) Herald."

Mr. Beaudry's style is simple and vivacious, calm and dig nified. He tells a plain story, void of passion, and unmarred by any language which could give offence.

From "The Religious Herald," (Hartford, Conn.)

The book is interesting, and far more reliable than some of our best stories ; it is, in fact, a series of conversations between the author and members of his family. We took it up for family reading, and could hardly relinquish it until read through. It is of value to Protestants, and should be read by all before they consider themselves competent to speak upon this subject. In fact, we know of no class of readers to whom it would not be interesting. It is a living witness to the truth the Popish Church still holds, not sparingly pointing out its errors, and promptly and boldly holding up erroneous views held by Protestants concerning this Church.

No Romanist can refute its statements; in fact, several staunch Romanists are introduced as characters in the plot of the story. It is furthermore full of charity for the errors of all men. God's service will surely be done by an extensive circulation of the work. It should go into every Sabbath-school in the land. It should be in every family, especially those employing Romanist domestics. Most of our best servants would read the work and be much profited by the same.

From "*The Richmond (Va.) Christian Advocate.*"

This is a timely book, and we hope will do much toward showing the true character and aims of the Romanists. The style is pleasing. The points of difference between Protestants and Catholics are strongly and clearly brought out, and the very language of Catholic writers is given, so that there can be no charge of misstatement. We hope this little book will be extensively read. It must do good.

From "*L'Aurore,*" (*French Protestant Weekly, Montreal, Canada.*)

This work, written in the form of conversations, is as admirable for its style as for the Christian spirit which characterizes it. It brings forth the principal errors of the Romish Church with clearness, without doing violence, however, to the religious sentiments of its Romish readers. By means of this book—unique of its kind—Mr. Beaudry has rendered a great service to the cause of the Gospel. Every Protestant engaged in evangelizing his Roman Catholic neighbours will find this work of inestimable value.

From "*The Ladies' Repository.*"

Mr. Beaudry promises to continue the conversations with his children at some future time. Should he do so, we cordially hope that the generous reception accorded to the present interesting work may induce him to place another volume in the hands of the publishers. The book before us breathes a catholicity of spirit rarely witnessed in those who have become converts to a faith not theirs by birthright. "Spiritual Struggles" is no misnomer. Love for the Romish Church ; a sincere belief in her infallibility ; a desire to prove the foundation of his faith, combined with an ardent affection for his mother, caused our author weary months of painful watchings, fastings, and prayers, ere he was willing to yield obedience to the voice of the Holy Spirit.

From " The N.Y. Daily Witness."

This book meets a felt want in the Christian world. "There are," as Professor Hawley remarks in his preface, "many volumes purporting to be narratives of personal experience and revelations of Catholic atrocity, but the style and spirit in which they are commonly written preclude their wide circulation and impede their usefulness."

The gentle spirit of charity in which this memoir is written, the full concession of sincerity to priests and people, the story of the agony and indecision through which its subject passed, all fit it to soften, impress, and prepare the mind for a thoughtful discussion of the points of controversy, making it at the same time a most desirable book to place in the hands of young Protestants. The evident truthfulness and circumstantiality of the narrative will interest old and young alike.

From " The Morning Star."

"Spiritual Struggles of a Roman Catholic" gives an account of the experience of Rev. Louis N. Beaudry in emerging from the traditional errors and religious superstitions of Romanism to the liberties of the gospel of Christ. The author has been for some time an accepted preacher of the Protestant faith, and in comparing the two religions he draws on an experience which in both cases has been deep and valuable. It throws considerable light on questions now agitating the public mind.

TESTIMONIALS.

From " The Canadian Methodist Magazine."

The spirit of this book is admirable. The author brings no railing accusation. He writes more in sorrow than in anger, and on controversial points cites the authority of recognized Romish manuals of religion. He points out many excellences in the Romish system, and some things worthy of Protestant imitation, especially the sedulous religious training of the young in the tenets of the Church. It is this that makes it so difficult to overcome the influence of these teachings, which have become enfibred in the very soul. The religious struggles of those who do break through these influences, and assert their unshackled liberty of conscience and responsibility to God alone, are oftentimes exceedingly severe. All the mechanical religious exercises that the author underwent brought no peace to his awakened conscience. The wearing of scapulars, performing of penances, frequent confession and frequent communion, did not heal the rankling wound he felt in his soul. It was only the application of the balm of Gilead and of the blood that cleanseth, that made him whole.

From " The Christian Guardian " (Toronto).

The book is written in an admirable spirit, and is calculated to do much good. It brings no railing accusation against Rome, but simply tells how one who was caught in the toils of her superstitions struggled into the liberty of the Gospel. Mr. Beaudry was the son of French-Canadian parents, and himself long resided in Lower Canada. The book illustrates the workings of the mystery of iniquity in a very instructive manner. The very pillars of our commonweal are imperilled by this system, which possesses such political power and such a comprehensive organization. Every Christian and patriot may learn lessons of deepest importance by the study of the presentation of the Romanism here set forth.

From " The Canadian Spectator " (Montreal).

The Rev. Mr. Beaudry is a convert from Romanism, who, unlike most "verts," is not given over to the "odium theologicum" in discussing the tenets of his former faith in comparison with Protestantism, but presents what he now conceives to be its errors in a manner that is remarkable for its fairness and kind treatment. The story of his difficulties and the way in which he found an escape from them is told in a series of conversations with his family and some friends, which from their easy style avoid the obtrusiveness of personal narration, and awake interest in the application made by the hearers of Mr. Beaudry's experience. Not the least valuable part of his treatment of Romanism and its contradictions is the amount of correct information as to its real teaching and his condemnation of vulgar errors in this respect—errors too frequently persisted in by even the most intelligent Protestants. Nevertheless, while speaking with all kindness and respect, his argument is plain and forcible, its arrangement skilful, and the illustrations apt. Additional interest attaches to the book from the fact that its author, though born in Vermont, is of a French-Canadian family.

From J. WARREN MARTIN, ESQ., *Chatham, Ont.*

The book is received and read all through with much interest. I have read several such works, but none have left on my mind and heart such prayerful yearning, love and pity for our Roman Catholic co-religionists. I am determined to know nothing among them but " Christ and Him crucified " henceforth, God being my helper.

From " The Wesleyan " (*Halifax*).

Having read this narrative, we can most heartily recommend it. As a rule we avoid books consisting of a series of conversations—they are too often insipid. This, by Mr. Beaudry, is a marked exception ; the conversational style only lends to it a deeper interest. It soon takes the reader captive, and holds him till he has perused its pages. The book is not a mere narrative ; its temperate tone and clearly-presented arguments, clinched with passages from Holy Scripture, render it an armory, by resort to which one may be prepared to meet all the arguments advanced in support of Roman Catholicism. Several

b

copies ought at once to be placed in each Sunday-school library. Our young people would read it, and in these days of danger be blessed by it.

From " The Star " (Montreal).

This book is entitled to, and, in all probability, will receive more favour at the hands of the public than other works of similar import.* * *

From " The Herald " (Montreal).

The case is presented with a fairness and moderation that is not often found in polemical works, and upon this characteristic Mr. Beaudry may be congratulated. The book is ably written, and we have no doubt that it will be read with much interest. To young students of theology it is especially valuable.

From " The Witness " (Montreal).

In these conversations is given what may be called an inside view of Romanism, which is quite remarkable for its candour, impartiality, and loving charity towards those who are in bonds by one who has been bound with them. There is no controversial bitterness in the book, which is, therefore, well adapted to win thoughtful minds to the truth.* * * * *

From " The Gazette " (Montreal).

While the author is thoroughly independent in the discussion of points of difference between his former and present creeds, he indulges in none of the angry and abusive language to which proselytes are only too prone. The narrative form which he has chosen gives it an interest and a claim on the attention of the ordinary reader, which dry theological argument would fail to produce. In the United States, where it was first published, the work elicited praise from the press of nearly all Christian communions. The book is neatly got up, and the frontispiece is a handsome likeness of Mr. Beaudry.

Yours in the Truth
Louis N. Beaudry.

SPIRITUAL STRUGGLES

OF A

ROMAN CATHOLIC:

An Autobiographical Sketch.

BY LOUIS N. BEAUDRY,

Author of " Army and Prison Experiences with the Fifth New York Cavalry."

WITH AN INTRODUCTION BY THE REV. B. HAWLEY, D.D

"Now rest, my long-divided heart;
Fixed on this blissful centre, rest;
Nor ever from thy Lord depart:
With Him of every good possessed."
—DODDRIDGE.

FOURTH CANADIAN EDITION, ENLARGED AND IMPROVED.

TORONTO:
WILLIAM BRIGGS,
78 & 80 KING STREET EAST.
MONTREAL: 3 BLEURY STREET.

1882.

TO MY

DISTINGUISHED SCHOOL-MATE,

THE REV. JOSEPH COOK,

THROUGH WHOSE INSTRUMENTALITY I WAS FIRST BROUGHT
IN CONTACT WITH THE SIMPLE WORD OF TRUTH,

AND TO

THE REV. BENJAMIN POMEROY,

BY WHOSE EVANGELISTIC LABOURS I WAS FINALLY LED TO
THE HAPPY EXPERIENCE OF SAVING FAITH
IN THE SURE PROMISE,

This Volume is most Affectionately Inscribed.

LOUIS N. BEAUDRY.

INTRODUCTION.

OF the many subjects now agitating the minds of the people in all Christian and civilized countries, none possesses a more weighty interest than that of Romanism in its relations to the civil and religious conditions of society. Everywhere and always the same, it seems now, as ever, antagonistic to the largest *personal* liberty, as also to the highest degree of intelligence and purity of a community. Not less opposed is it to any clear convictions of personal *responsibility* to God and a good government. These are facts that are now well and widely known. Christianly enlightened communities and States are somewhat awake to them, and are more or less active in securing relief from them. Scholarly and popular writers are flooding the world with light on these subjects. Volumes are written and libraries are enriched by exposures and histories of what seems to us a dangerous error. Every new phase of the system, as civilization and Christianity advance, is being put in its true light. Of these things there may be, thus far, little or no lack of information. But there is another aspect in which the *animus*, the genius, and the workings of Romanism may be seen. Though there are now and then defections from nominal Christianity to Papacy, there are also, and in greater numbers, converts from Romanism to vital Christianity. And of these there have been thus far but few readable developments in an attractive or permanent form. The transition in any such case is always great. The struggles to emerge from traditional errors and religious superstitions are, for reasons obvious to all who have studied the genius of Papal teachings and errors, not unfrequently severe, and even heroic. And any one who has passed through them, and has the power and the will to detail them in an attractive form, meets by so doing a *desideratum*.

Such a book, not cumbersome, not dull, nor written in the ordinary style of history, or even of narrative, but one that traces out delicately and carefully the workings of the soul in its religious transition, is needed. Families in which Romish domestics are employed need such a book written from the stand-point of experience. Young people who see and are favourably impressed by the higher intelligence and purer morality of Protestant Christianity, as also of Christian countries, and especially those who desire to read the Holy Scriptures that they may know for themselves the truth as it is in Jesus, need such a book. But where shall they find it? Volumes, purporting to be narratives of personal experience and revelations of Catholic atrocities, there are in sufficient numbers; but the style and spirit in which they are commonly written preclude their wide circulation, or, if circulated, prevent any wide usefulness.

Having had the privilege of reading, with much care and pleasure, a volume in manuscript entitled "Spiritual Struggles," written by Rev. Louis N. Beaudry, a convert from Romanism, and for many years an intelligent, pious, and useful Christian minister, which seems to me well calculated to be popular and useful, and, indeed, to meet a felt want in the Church, I am pleased to commend it to the reading public. It is not only, as it purports, an auto-biography—which all who know the writer will esteem to be of itself a commendation—but it gives in a series of conversations, and, therefore, in familiar style, the struggles of others who were participants in the family *séances*, and who by these means were gradually, intelligently, and religiously led to freedom in Christ.

The several chapters seem to me to sustain throughout a natural and philosophical relation to each other ; and though the autobiography in fact does not clearly appear as is usual, in the first few pages, yet the writer is all the while the central person, giving character and direction to the conversations. Drawn out in due time to give his own experience, he proceeds to do so without marring the familiar style of the work. The plan of arrangement is unique, simple, artistic, and gradually revealing, so as to keep the reader on the *qui vive* of interest and expectancy up to the point where the narrative of personal experience begins, and that is harmoniously continued with the freshness of Romance to the very close, when "rest is found—rest to the weary soul."

Much of the beauty and attractiveness of the volume lies in the very natural and easy manner in which is shown how the writer, and some of those associated with him in the *séances*, were led by the truth and the Spirit of God out of the doubts and errors in which they had been educated to a clear experience and appreciation of justification through faith. And so precious did their experience become, that each and all, young and old, were led to an entire renunciation of the traditions of men, and to a full embrace of the truths of the Gospel.

Readers of the volume will see how other persons in similar conditions of error may be led to a like precious faith.

The practical lessons for all who would be, in a similar way, instrumental in leading the erring to Christ, that are gathered from the book, are, that kindness, tenderness, a spirit of concession, and according to others all that truth and justice will allow, and an admission that all truth is exclusively with no one sect, accompanied by a disposition to reason together, will go far to do away prejudice and to win souls to Jesus.

Because of these and other considerations, I cheerfully and strongly commend the book to the reading public. In many respects it is suited to juvenile readers, and will be a welcome volume in the libraries of Sunday-schools and of families.

BOSTWICK HAWLEY.

CONTENTS.

Spiritual Struggles of a Roman Catholic.

I.

FACE TO FACE—MISS LUELLA—SURPRISES—THE PLAN
—NORA.

Come now, let us reason together.—Isaiah.

T was a lovely Sabbath afternoon, early in the autumn of 18—. I had just returned to the parsonage from an interesting session of our Sunday-School, where I had been making a few remarks, contrasting the privileges of the children before me with my own, when I was a child. I was now seated in an easy chair in my study, absorbed in pensive reveries.

> "The melancholy days had come,
> The saddest of the year."

The cricket was just beginning his solemn chirpings in the walls around me, and directly before my window the leaves of the drooping elms gave evident signs of decay and approaching winter. Here and there among the leaves were irregular openings, through which, like rifts in the clouds that reveal the blue sky beyond, I could distinctly see the placid bosom of the noble Hudson, now beautifully emblematic of a soul peacefully resting by faith in the promises of the world's Redeemer. But while I looked and pondered, a steamer, plying between two neighbouring cities, laden with her crowd of pleasure-seekers and Sabbath-breakers, disturbed the glassy surface of the stream, and interrupted the pleasing flow of my meditations.

Just then two loving arms were thrown around my neck, and, as I slightly turned my head, a sweet kiss was bestowed upon my lips. It was Luella, my eldest child, now almost a young lady, who, seeing my study door ajar, had softly tripped in on tiptoe behind me, to surprise me with her caresses. Seating herself in her camp-chair by my side, and looking up inquiringly into my face, she remarked :

"Why, father, we were not a little astonished to-day at your telling us that you were *nineteen years old* when you first went into one of our Sunday-schools! For my part, I should like to know the reason why you did not begin to attend Sunday-school as young as we did,' meaning, of course, herself, her brother Johnnie, and her little sister Mary.

"Now, Luella, I suppose that you have already learned the answer to your question, at least in a general way; which is, that I was educated in the faith of the Roman Catholic Church. But I perceive by the tone of your question, and the deep solicitude expressed in your countenance, that you are anxious to learn the *particulars* of my peculiar and eventful life, especially during its earlier years."

"You have guessed it exactly, father; but I did not know that I could express so much by a mere accent, or a look of my face and eyes."

"You have many things yet to learn, my child. I hope your teachers may themselves be so well instructed as not only to be able to satisfy the natural inquisitiveness of your mind, and to develop all its latent faculties, but also so evangelical in spirit as to lead you into that beautiful Christian experience, the beginning and progress of which may be at least intimated by the simple words: *penitence, pardon, peace, purity, power.*"

"O, greatly as I desire to know more and more of the ways of God, I am very glad to be able to tell you that I think I know something of these subjects already, dear father."

Rising as she spoke, she again warmly threw

her arms around me, and sobbed on my bosom,
while I pressed her closely to my heart, praising
God for the saving mercies which were so freely
bestowed on myself and family. At length,
after wiping away my tears of joy, as also her
own, she resumed her seat, and I continued :—

" For several reasons, Luella, I am glad this
subject of my religious struggles has come up to-
day. In the first place, it gives me a good opportunity to say, with the royal psalmist, ' Come
and hear, all ye that fear God, and I will declare
what he hath done for my soul.' And again,
like the man whom Jesus had saved, I may go
home to my friends and tell them what great
things the Lord hath done for me, and hath had
compassion on me. I trust, too, that I may be
impelled and controlled by the disposition enjoined by the Apostle Peter upon his brethren
to ' be ready always to give an answer to every
man that asketh you a reason of the hope that
is in you, with meekness and fear.'

" I suppose you are aware that this question
of Romanism is just now awakening a deep
solicitude in the popular mind of every civilized
nation, and especially of our own. It is being
discussed on the platform, in the pulpit, and by
the press, from nearly every stand-point possible, and not seldom by those who are ignorant
of its principles and spirit, and who in not a

few cases evince quite other than Christian
sentiments. As to myself, I am conscious of no
feelings of hostility toward any man or class of
men. I know, too, that 'hard words are like
hailstones in summer, beating down and de-
stroying what they would nourish were they
melted into drops.' So, in speaking to you or
to others on this subject, my only motive is to
do good and to advance the cause of truth ; and
in this case I can speak, as you know, from the
depths of experience, of the things which I have
seen and known.

"You have often heard me express a strong
desire to get Romanists and Protestants to hear
and read with candour one another's views, or,
were it possible, to reason together, assured that,
would they do so, much of the misunderstanding
between them would soon cease, political animosities would be removed, religious courtesies
would be freely exchanged, and no contention
would exist among us, save that noble rivalry,
or rather emulation, to see who can best work
and best agree. All men would feel better
pleased with themselves and those around them
if only they were better acquainted with each
other. How important, too, in a land like ours,
especially where the population is made up of
all nationalities, with all degrees of intellectual, social, and moral development, with all

2

shades of political and religious creeds, that men should meet and consult with one another, for in this way only shall we learn that no man is either wholly right or wholly wrong; and under the force of such a conviction the truth will be sought and found, and we may here witness the fulfillment of Isaiah's beautiful prophecy, 'The wolf also shall dwell with the lamb, and the leopard shall lie down with the kid; and the calf and the young lion and the fatling together; and a little child shall lead them,' even the holy child Jesus.

"Now, toward the achievement of such a grand and glorious realization I have many years been desirous of contributing my mite of influence; and for a long time, and especially of late, have I seriously thought of writing a book, by means of which I might help to bring my Roman Catholic and Protestant friends and fellow-citizens face to face, as it were, to discuss in a friendly and Christian spirit the matters which have kept them so long and so widely at variance. And this I can do in answering your question. Really, I begin to feel as if this sub-ject had come up between us to-day, Luella, just in time to stimulate me to undertake this work, and to assist me in its prosecution"

"Well, well, I had no idea of putting in motion such a train of events when I asked you my question."

"I told you before, that there is much yet for you to learn. But how would you like to have our private conversation made the subject of a public chronicle?"

"Why, indeed, you make my head whirl by your surprises! You don't mean to have printed in a book what we are now talking about, so that *everybody* may read it, do you?"

"Would you object?"

"I scarcely know what to answer, you take me so off my guard."

"Well, no matter now. I have a new proposition to make right here."

"Another surprise, I suppose!"

"Perhaps so, but it is simply this:—that you run downstairs and call in the rest of the children, for you know they are very fond of hearing us tell stories, and I think this one is not above their capacity. Invite your mother and Aunt Melie also, if they think that baby Charlie will not disturb them by his crowing or crying."

"Shall I not ask Nora to come in too?"

"I think not now, for she might take it as an offence, or 'a bit of persecution,' as she would call it."

Nora was a sincere Romanist, born in this country of Irish parents; but she was not an

ordinary servant girl. Her father, once a wealthy
merchant, had spared no pains nor expense in
her domestic and general education. But bank-
ruptcy had brought the family to want. Being
naturally of an independent and somewhat peculiar disposition, she had strangely chosen her
portion in household duties. Her contact, for a
few months, with the general class of kitchen-
maids, had given her their characteristic and
distinctive dialect and manners. This, however,
was only when she seemed to forget herself ; for
she was capable of filling the place of a cultured
lady. Though but a short time in our family,
we had all become much attached to her and she
to us.

This proposition just suited Luella, and awaᴊ
she glided like a bird.

II.

FIRST SEANCE — SINCERITY — SUNDAY-SCHOOLS—SATIS-
FIED AND NOT SATISFIED—CHARITY AND UNITY.

**And now abideth faith, hope, charity, these three; but the greatest of
these is charity—***Paul.*

IT did not take Luella long to inform the
family of the interesting juncture of
affairs in the study, and soon I heard the
rapid footfalls of the children on the
stairs, followed by the mother and the
aunt. Meanwhile I had brought in chairs from
the adjoining rooms to accommodate them all,
and presently the place became the scene of life
and interest. Even the *baby* seemed to enjoy it
greatly.

In a few words the object of our interview
was explained, and then I suggested that in accordance with my usual custom, taken from that
of the Christians of old, we ought to begin this
interesting subject with religious devotions; for
St. Paul writes to Timothy, "I exhort, therefore
that *first of all*, supplications, prayers, interces-

sions, and giving of thanks be made *for all men.*
We then knelt together, and repeated slowly
and solemnly, in concert, the prayer of prayers,
namely, " Our Father, which art in heaven, hallowed be thy name. Thy kingdom come. Thy
will be done in earth as it is in heaven. Give us
this day our daily bread. And forgive us our
trespasses as we forgive them that trespass
against us. And lead us not into temptation,
but deliver us from evil. For thine is the kingdom, and the power, and the glory, for ever.
Amen."

On resuming our seats, Mary remarked,
" Why, father, this is what we say together
every morning at the time of prayers."

" Yes, my dear ; it is the Lord's prayer, and it
is in the spirit of this prayer that we must feel
and act through all the day and in all things ;
and we have said it now that we may be especially guided by the Lord in what we are about
to say."

Then addressing myself to the whole company, I remarked, that as certain classes even of
heathens were accustomed to take their children
out immediately after birth, and turn their faces
toward the open sky, that their first impressions
might be of heaven and of grandeur, so I desired
that my children in their earliest years should
be taught God's holy, saving truth, that they

might learn to think and feel properly toward
all mankind, and act accordingly. Indeed, the
great Teacher said, that the duty of every Christian is comprehended in these two commandments, "Thou shalt love the Lord thy God with
all thy heart, and thy neighbour as thyself."

"Now," I continued, "I am aware that it is
very natural that two religious sects as distinct
as are Romanists and Protestants in their manner of life and modes of worship should misun-
derstand each other, especially when a long
history of antagonisms, sometimes more or less
bloody, urges them to further animosities. But
while their views on certain controverted subjects are diametrically opposed, there are many
others in which they perfectly agree—and these
are vital subjects—though other matters of difference lie within debatable ground, and yet are
such as they might be made to agree in by reasoning together. You will probably understand
me better when I bring before you some of these
latter subjects. For instance, it is no uncommon
thing to hear a Protestant charging a Romanist
with being insincere in his profession of what
he calls 'his faith.'"

"Insincere!" almost shouted two or three
voices.

"How can they be sincere," inquired Luella,
"and believe such things as are generally re-

ported of them, and even affirmed in their own books ?"

"Now, now, children; this is very much like what I feared of you. You have not received this spirit from me, however; and I am glad of the opportunity of removing this prejudice and I suspect, other similar ones, from your minds I assure you that *no class of people are more sincere in their beliefs.* The facts which I can adduce to establish the truthfulness of this statement are very numerous. Look first at the devotion of Romish parents in *teaching their children* the doctrines and practices of the 'Holy Mother Church,' as they call her. No sect, either religious or otherwise, takes more pains to indoctrinate the young. Their children, generally when only a few days old, are taken to their churches and baptized. They are then considered members of the Church. As soon as they are able to speak, they are taught to repeat the prayers of the Church and the Catechism, which contains their doctrines. This is done with untiring industry and generally with great solemnity. When they are sufficiently grown up they are sent to the schools of the Church, which are always in the hands of nuns or 'sisters,' or of others who devote all their time and energy to this work."

"But would you recommend these schools or

convents as proper places to send *our* children for instruction?" asked Mrs. Beaudry, with considerable feeling.

"I have not said anything of the kind; nor have I time now to say just what I think about these institutions; but at the same time I am convinced that by these and other means Romanism is doing vastly more for her children in her way than is Protestantism."

"Indeed, father," said Johnnie, his dark eye flashing with emotion, "and were you not a Protestant when you had us baptized? and are you not constantly teaching us in the Sunday-school and at home the Catechism and the Discipline of our Church?"

"Certainly; but this practice is not as general among Protestants as among Romanists."

"But are not our Sunday-schools doing as much for us as Roman Catholics are doing for their children?"

"Only in part, my child; and yet many parents among us leave the religious training of their children wholly to the Sunday-school. But you must remember that the family circle is before the Sunday-school, not only in point of time, but also of importance. The parent is the child's first and most influential teacher. You ought to know what a little boy once said when some one was contradicting him about a certain doctrine."

" What was it ?" Johnnie quickly asked.

" O, simply this ; he clinched his argument by saying, 'It's true, for ma says so ; and if ma says so, it's so *if it aint so.*' Now, this labour of Romish parents for their children proves their sincerity."

I see the point and acknowledge the force of the argument," said Luella, "and I see it is doing us good to reason thus together."

" Let us reason, then, a little further. *Witness the fidelity of Romanists to the rules and devotions of their Church.* They fast often and much. They keep every year a forty days' Lent, in imitation, as they say, of Christ's forty days' fast in the wilderness of Judea, and in commemoration of His passion ; and because the Church ordains it, they abstain from all 'flesh meats' on Fridays—it used to be on Fridays and Saturdays also."

" Well, this is not a little curious," interrupted Aunt Melie, "that such an ordinance was ever altered in a Church which professes to never change."

" That makes me think," added Luella, " of their Church motto, which I read in one of their books. It is '*Semper eadem,*' which means, as I found by my Latin lexicon, 'Always the same.'"

" I am glad to seé that you remember so well what you read, and that you are learning your Latin lessons so thoroughly; but I have not time now to explain these changes to you, for I fear we shall lose the thread of the argument. I must continue to give you the proofs of their sincerity. *See how strict they are in attending the services of their Church.* On the Sabbath they are up early and away to Church, though many of them have much to do and far to go, and you can hear the tramping of their feet on the walks while most other people are asleep in their beds. Their churches are crowded at nearly every service, and a marked degree of devotion is observable in most of the worshippers. I well remember when myself, with my brothers and other Romish friends of the neighbourhood used to go to church nine miles afoot, through mud or dust, because we felt that it was our duty. Was that no sign of sincerity? We certainly showed our faith by our works."

" Surely," responded Mrs. Beaudry, "such examples of devotion ought to put to shame the many delinquents in our different Protestant denominations, and should provoke them to love and to good works."

" But are they not thus attentive to *external* duties," asked Aunt Melie, "because they are taught to expect the salvation of their souls through such means ? "

" You must judge for yourself when I have presented to you other facts bearing upon this subject.   But I have not finished my argument in vindication of their sincerity.   I wish to give you at least another illustration of it.   It is found in *their attachment to the Church of their fathers.*   When I was nineteen years of age, just before the event of my first going to a Sunday-school—a matter referred to in Luella's introductory question to me to-day—had any man stepped up to me, and presenting a pistol to my head, said, ' You must be a Protestant now, or I will take your life,' I would have replied without any hesitation or evasion whatever, ' Take my life, sir, but my integrity never.'   Martyrdom would have been cheerfully accepted rather than separation from the Church.   And thousands of Romanists, I am sure, feel just as I did then."

" I see clearly that you were more to be pitied than blamed," said Johnnie; adding with emphasis, " and I'm sure we will never charge Roman Catholics again with the sin of insincerity."

" But may not this attachment to the Church, which is generally commendable, go so far, at times at least, as to become sinful and hurtful?" asked Mrs. Beaudry.

"Undoubtedly; for men may be sincere in an error, and we ought to prefer truth before party or sect, and be attached to a Church only so far as it teaches and practises the truth as it is in Jesus. The great Apostle Paul wrote to his Corinthian brethren, 'Be ye followers of me, even as I also am of Christ,' showing that he was to be followed *only as* he followed Christ, and not otherwise. But then the masses of the people have very little inclination—if, indeed, they are not wanting in time and ability—to search out the truth for themselves, and they, therefore, become as strongly attached to what they are *told* is truth, as the truly studious do to the truth itself. And you may be sure that no external or physical force will ever change their belief or convert their souls. 'Faith cometh by hearing, and hearing by the word of God.'"

"The fault, then, must be in their priests," said Aunt Melie; "and judging them by a sample which came under my own observation once, I have always believed them insincere and hypocritical."

"That is undoubtedly true of some of them, but I will show you that it is not true of all. Your suspicions will fall to the ground when I produce even but a few facts of history. Their extensive missionary labours alone refute the charge. Look, too, at their great Church enterprises; their laborious and successful educational efforts—successful at least, from their own point of view—and their vast charitable institutions for the aged, the vagrant, the orphan, and the poor."

"But does not their system of religion *produce*, at least, in part, the poverty and wretchedness which these institutions are designed to relieve? Is not this to use the old proverb, 'robbing Peter to pay Paul?'"

"That may all be true; and yet it does not disprove their sincerity, for many of them have suffered even martyrdom for their faith."

"I cannot yet see how this can be," she continued.

"You will have no difficulty in seeing it when you trace out the leading facts of their education and training from childhood to priesthood. They are first consecrated to this one object of life; then nurtured in the teachings and discipline of the Church; put into the schools under the absolute control of the 'brothers' and 'fathers;' kept from all contact with the active outside world; forbidden to study, or even read, any book which could possibly prejudice their minds against the Church or any of her interpretations, as you can see by consulting the

In·lex Librorum Prohibitorum et Expurgan-dorum."

" O, what do you mean by those long words ?" inquired Johnnie.

Taking down my large Webster's Dictionary, and handing it to Luella, I told her to look for the word "*Index*," under which she read as follow : " In the Roman Catholic Church the Index Prohibitory is a catalogue of books which are forbidden to be read ; the Index Expurgatory is a catalogue specifying passages in books which are to be expunged or altered. These catalogues are published, with additions, from time to time, under the sanction of the Pope."

Returning the Dictionary to the table, I remarked, " The spirit which animates their education and controls it may be seen further in an address recently made by the Roman Pontiff himself to the students of one of the papal colleges. Here is one of the emphatic sentences : ' Let us hasten to cultivate sanctity of life by attending to studies, by obedience to superiors, by frequenting the sacraments, and by not disturbing ourselves with what occurs in the world ; by *never having in our hand any daily newspaper*, but especially those journals verily issuing from the depths of hell, which, if one shall take in his hand he will be guilty of **a** grievous fault.' "

"Is this the way these clerical students are in-structed? Now," continued Aunt Melie, "I am satisfied that I was wrong in suspecting them as a class, of insincerity."

"Yes, indeed; and finally, endowed with holy orders from the authorities of the college at Maynooth, Ireland, or of some other approved institute or university, they come forth fully believing themselves to be in the sacred succession of the Apostles of our Lord, with 'the keys of the kingdom of heaven' in their hands, so that 'whatsoever they shall bind on earth shall be bound in heaven, and whatsoever they shall loose on earth shall be loosed in heaven.' I have been personally acquainted with several priests both in Canada and in the United States, and I am satisfied that many of them are quite sincere."

"Their sincerity is further seen in their almost constant practice of devotions, in observing what is called the 'Church Office,' which is a form of prayer consisting of psalms, lessons, hymns, &c., used by all the clergy, and by the religious of both sexes in the Romish Church. This Office is divided into seven parts, commonly called the 'Seven Canonical Hours,' commencing with the matins, or midnight office, and ending with the compline, at the close of day."

"Is this what the priests and nuns are busy

with," asked Luella, "when we see them on the boats or in the cars? for their lips are almost constantly in motion, as if they were trying to whisper something, or they are reading from a little book which I think I have heard you call a 'breviary,' or prayer-book."

"That's it exactly. These devotions consume a large portion of the day."

"But, Louis," asked Mrs. Beaudry, "do you really believe that they are sincere when they ask and receive money of their people for the pardon of their sins?"

"It is not true—as it seems to me I must have told you before this time—that they do any such thing, at least in this country. It does appear, from certain writers, that it must have been true in other countries and other ages; but of this I am sure, that no money was ever asked of me by any priest in the confessional, though I have often been there and was never refused 'absolution.' In case the priest does not know the penitent who presents himself for confession, he inquires whether he contributes anything towards the support of the Church. If the individual has failed to do so in the past, and refuses to pledge himself to do so in the future, the priest refuses to hear his confession, and he is justly regarded as unworthy of any of the privileges of the Church."

3

"But how is it that Romish servants, just before going to their Church, want so much money, as you know Nora does nearly every Sabbath?"

"I am aware that this might give rise to the suspicion that money is used in the confessional, for, in order to secure it, some servants present this as their plea. But you must consider that the priests make *other* demands upon their people. Think of the vast and costly edifices they erect, always in the most conspicuous and expensive localities, and often, too, in communities where they have very few, if any, wealthy communicants. Whenever the priests call on them for contributions for a private or public enterprise, Roman Catholics, rich and poor, pour out their money like water. I have known families who, by contributing, as they were urged by their spiritual guides, have reduced themselves to such destitution as to be compelled to seek aid from the town or county where they resided. Napoleon Roussel has styled theirs the 'religion of money.' It is undeniably true in more respects than one; but they do not pay money for the pardon of sins, as you have thought."

"But does not their doctrine of Purgatory involve principles which have led us and many others into this belief?" Mrs. Beaudry asked.

"Very likely. Concerning this doctrine, however, I expect to tell you by-and-by more than I have time to say to you now."

Then taking from the table a little book, entitled "Grounds of the Roman Catholic Doctrine,
contained in the Profession of Faith," published
by Pope Pius IV., I turned to page 4f, and read :
"*Of Purgatory.*—What is the doctrine of the
Church as to this point ?"

"*Answer.* We constantly hold that there is a
Purgatory, and that the souls therein detained
are helped by the suffrages of the faithful : that
is, by the prayers and alms offered for them, and
principally by the holy sacrifice of the Mass."

"We are further told," I continued, "that the
prayers of the priest must be obtained in addition to those of the people, for which he must
be paid money, as also for the saying of masses,
and that thereby the sins of the souls in purgatory are remitted unto them. From these premises many have reasoned as follows : 'Now, if
the priest is paid money to secure the pardon of
sins *in Purgatory,* does it not follow that he is
also paid for the pardon of sins *in the confessional ?'* Every one must admit that your reasoning is perfectly logical, and these facts shield
you from the charge of having accused the
Romanists without cause. The same process of
reasoning may be applied, with equal force, to the
doctrine of indulgences."

"Really, father," asked Luella, "do you think
you can name any more points in which Protest-

ants, and even your own family, have erroneously
charged the Roman Catholics ?"

"Yes, my child; here is one: I have somtimes
heard Protestants say that Roman Catholic theo-
lógy or teaching is wholly heterodox, or false.
This book, called 'Grounds,' etc., from which I
just read, will repel this charge."   After reading
a few pages I said, "Now you see that every es-
sential doctrine taught in the Protestant Churches
is also taught in the Romish Churches.   The
Apostle's Creed, which is really an epitome of
the Gospels, is repeated and believed in all
Churches, both Roman Catholic and Protestant,
throughout the world, without varying even a
word or syllable.   The Lord's Prayer—and what
prayer is better entitled to universal usage, being
the only prayer our blessed Saviour ever taught
to his Disciples, an epitome of prayers ?—is daily
repeated in nearly all the languages of the world,
and by all professed Christians.   If Romanists
would only stop here, and not try to add to that
which is divinely perfect, all our religious differences would at once vanish.   I am free, however, to say that there is enough good and sound
doctrine in the Roman Catholic Church, if properly studied and applied, to save the world."

"Do you mean to say, father," asked Johnnie
quite excitedly, "that any Papists are saved ?"

"Most certainly.   I believe that some in that

Church, like Madame Guyon and Bishop Fénelon—grasping the saving truth which they have been taught, and assisted by the Holy Spirit, who, like the pure sunlight which floods the earth this afternoon, is diffused throughout the world—enjoy much of the favour of God, walk in all the light they have, to the full measure of their responsibilities, and rejoice in hope of heaven."

"But I am convinced," added Aunt Melie, "that while this *may* be the happy experience of some, the masses are entangled in the meshes of error, sink the spirit and power of true religion in the mere ceremony and outward form, and follow the commandments and traditions of men rather than the word of God."

"But do you think these Roman Catholics are really satisfied with their religion?" inquired Johnnie.

"They are, and yet they are not."

"Why, your answer is something of a riddle."

"Then let me explain it. They believe and profess that they have true faith, and are in the true Church. This is a conviction of the intellect, and comes from human teaching—from their parents and priests. With this the majority of them are satisfied. But when they look at their moral state; when they search for that kingdom of heaven which our blessed Saviour

says, ' is within us,' and which the Apostle Paul
describes as being 'not meat and drink, *but
righteousness, and peace, aud joy in the Holy
Ghost,*' they are not satisfied with their condition, and, like the poet, they sigh,—

> " 'Break off the yoke of inbred sin,
>   And fully set my spirit free ;
> I cannot rest till pure within—
>   Till I am wholly lost in thee.'

But this rest for which the spirit pants is a
matter of moral consciousness, and can be obtained or wrought within, only through the
agency of the Holy Spirit, who is freely given to
us in the redemption of Jesus Christ."

"This reminds me," said Johnnie, " of the precious words of Jesus himself, '*Come unto me,*
all ye that labour and are heavy-laden, and *l
will give you rest.* Take *my yoke* upon you
and *learn of me,* for I am meek and lowly in
heart, *and ye shall find rest unto your souls.*' "

"O, father, Jesus said," quickly added Mary.
Suffer the *little children to come unto me,* and
forbid them not, for of such is the kingdom of
God.' "

While they were repeating these beautiful
passages, Luella was gazing upon the smooth
surface of the river, and, when they ceased, she
exclaimed with animation,—

"See there ! I'm sure that's a good emblem of

this soul-rest!" Then turning to me, with her hand upon her breast, she continued, "And what is best of all, dear father, I feel it *here*, to-day, in my heart."

"I perceive," I said with emotion, " that we have gained something, both intellectually and spiritually, by our reasoning together. O, would that all men might not only reason with one another, but also with God, in the blessed assurance which the prophet gives, that though their 'sins be as scarlet, they shall be as white as snow ; though they be red like crimson, they shall be as wool.'"

As the last of these precious words fell from my lips, the clock below struck seven. How short the time had been ! Every one was sorry that we were compelled to close our interview so soon. Preparation had now to be made for the evening service at the church.

"Next Sabbath," said I, " the Lord willing we will meet again, and I will tell you some incidents of my childhood. But before we part, let us sing those beautiful words :—

> " ' Sweetly may we all agree,
> Touched with softest sympathy ;
> Kindly for each other care ;
> Every member feel its share.
> Many are we now and one,
> We who Jesus have put on :
> *Names, and sects, and parties fall :*
> *Thou, O Christ, art all in all.*'"

III.

MY CHILDHOOD—ANCESTORS—EVANGELINE OF ACADIA
—EARLY LESSONS, GOOD AND BAD—PROTESTANTS—
PUZZLED—PRIESTS AND PLAY—SUNDAY DESECRATION.

*When I was a child, I spake as a child, I understood as a child, I
thought as a child ; but when I became a man, I put away childish things.
—Paul.*

THE week had passed away but too
tardily, as the children thought, in their
great anxiety to hear my story. Many
times Mary, in her childish way, had
inquired : "Father, when will it be
Sunday afternoon again?" To me the time had
been sufficiently brief, being filled up with the
many calls and duties of an extensive parish.

The holy Sabbath came at length, but clouds
obscured the sky and threatened rain, which
indeed began to fall just before the afternoon
session of the Sunday-school. Consequently
the attendance was not quite as large nor the
exercises so long as usual. This enabled our
family group to assemble in the study a few
minutes earlier than on the Sabbath previous.

The scene without was greatly changed, but within all was animation and delight. Some one remarked that the elm looked rather tearful out there in the drenching rain, and that the heavens showed trouble as they groaned with muttering thunders and glowed with occasional lightning.

"But," interrupted Johnnie, "as much as I love to study the trees and flowers, I am more interested just now in father's story, and I propose that we sit still and let him go on." Then turning to me, he continued, "Father, you remember that last Sabbath you corrected us in our false ideas of Roman Catholics, for which I am glad, for I know that it has made me a better boy all the week, especially when I have been playing with Romish boys or talking with Nora in the kitchen. Now it seems to me, that, as you know both sides of this question, you ought to present here, and, if possible, show how to remove, the false views which they undoubtedly entertain toward Protestants. I am quite sure that Nora said several things to me about Protestants concerning which she must be mistaken."

"This is just the subject which I intend to present, my son; and it will fully appear as I proceed with my narrative, as you will presently see."

"That's right, father; give us the story any way," said Mary, and she came up to me and leaned on the arm of my chair.

"I'll begin now, then, if you'll give attention.

"I was born in the Town of Highgate, Franklin County, Vermont, August 11th, 1833, about one mile from Saxe's Mills. My parents were French, as you see by our name, and the French language was the first I ever spoke. One branch of the family was descended from a long line of warriors, which can be traced backward to the belligerent Franks of ancient Gaul. In modern times they fought in this country at Ticonderoga and Quebec, under the brave Montcalm, during what is known in American history as the French and Indian War. The other branch, on my mother's side, whose name was Marie Bail de Printemps, presents an almost uninterrupted succession of Roman Catholic religionists. Her grandmother was a fellow-sufferer of 'Evangeline,' the heroine of one of Longfellow's most beautiful poems, in which may be found a picture of the ardent, simple, religious spirit, and of the sufferings of those eighteen thousand Acadians who were driven from their loved country over the entire continent."

"But did you *always* live in Vermont?" asked Luella.

"When I was five years old my parents returned to Lower Canada, their native province, and settled in the town of Henryville, near Lake Champlain. After about six years' residence there, we again removed into my beloved Green Mountain State, and two years afterward to Ticonderoga, New York, where we remained several years. When I was about seven years of age I came near being drowned in the South River."

"What, father!" cried Johnnie, "just as I did some time ago in Kinderhook Creek?"

"Much like it, for I was barely saved from a watery grave."

"How good the Lord has been to us all!" exclaimed Luella. "Doubtless he has preserved our lives for some good purpose."

"I trust that none of us," I added, "will in anywise frustrate his designs; but that, as the poet Cowper has written, we may realize that though

"'The bud may have a bitter taste,
Sweet will be the flower.'

But I must continue my narrative. My mother was one of the most earnest and devoted Romanists I ever knew. Every member of her numerous family of fifteen—nine sons and six daughters—was baptized in early childhood. I was taken to the town of St. Mary, Province of

Quebec, a great many miles from home, to be baptized. Every one of us was also thoroughly trained in the teachings of the Church. I was taught many good lessons which I have never forgotten nor rejected, and for which I am truly grateful. The following were the leading principles inculcated—namely, that *religion is a subject of supreme importance;* that on awaking every morning I should say, 'My God, I give thee my heart;' that after dressing myself I should kneel down and offer my morning prayer; that I should partake of my meals with sobriety and temperance, and not without asking God's blessing upon them; that I should attend public religious services every day, if possible, and apply myself faithfully to my vocation in life, or daily labour; that I should assist the poor according to my means, and that every night I should examine my conscience and offer my evening prayer."

"Surely," said Luella, "this is just as good instruction as any child need receive, and all of it, I think, is perfectly scriptural."

"That is just the reason I continue to practice these things, and desire to do so till the day of my death. But while I was schooled in these wholesome Christian truths, I was also taught *to hate and shun Protestants.* More stress was laid upon this branch of my education, no doubt, because there were so many Protestants around us. I saw also that they were not permitted to bo buried in our cemeteries. In my early childhood, whenever I heard the sound of a Protestant bell a holy horror seemed to fill my soul, and I could have leaped for joy at seeing every Protestant church around us in flames."

"O, how wicked it was to feel like that!" exclaimed Johnnie, with sadness in his countenance.

"I know it now, but I did not think so then. You remember that Jesus went so far as to say to his Disciples, 'The time cometh that whosoever killeth you will think that he doeth God service.'"

"But *you* didn't feel like that—did you, father? for then you would have been a murderer."

"I was not very far from feeling so, I am ashamed to confess. But it is no wonder, for I was told that Protestantism is not only a denial and rejection of all spiritual religion, but a virtual crusade against it, and that inasmuch as the Romish Church is the only true one, whoever rejects it rejects God and his Christ, and must be regarded as a 'a heathen man and a publican.' This is an opinion entertained by all rigid Roman Catholics."

"O, I think it was this that Nora tried to tell me the other day," added Johnnie.

"My father used to say derisively that his old brindled ox was more pious than a Protestant, because the beast would always kn.eel before he lay down, which was much more than a Protestant would do."

"Is it possible that grandfather would talk in that way?" exclaimed Luella in surprise.

"That may be true of a vast body of Protestants who make no profession of *personal* or *experimental* religion, and live without prayer," said Aunt Melie. "I now see what terrible responsibility rests upon them in this matter. They are really the great stumbling-block in the way of the Gospel. But then it is a pity that your father had not fallen among a better class of Protestants."

"O, this view of the subject was drawn from his religious training rather than from observation," I remarked in explanation. "All this spite and ridicule is substantially taught in the Church Catechism,* from which I will translate a brief passage."

Turning to page 24, I read:—

"'Are there many Catholic Churches?'

"'No, the only Catholic is the Roman Church, *out of which there is no salvation.*'

* "Petit Catéchisme du Diocèse de Québec."

" 'What must we think of those other societies which call themselves Churches, but do not profess the same faith that we do, and are not subject to the same pastors ? '

" 'They are *human* institutions, which serve only to lead men astray, and cannot bring them to God.' "

Laying down the book I continued: " The commentary upon this passage—and no passage was more thoroughly taught and enforced—was that Protestantism, referred to here, protests against Christ and his Church, against all law and gospel. The word *Protestant* itself was made to mean all this. Therefore I was told that it was a grevions sin, and almost a sacrilege, to read a Protestant book, or to attend their meetings; and that I must shun them as Eve ought to have shunned the tempting serpent. This question is thoroughly discussed in one of the most popular books of instruction in the Church, where may be found the following passage:*

" 'What, if a person, through absolute necessity of his unhappy circumstances, should be tied to a place where he can never hear mass; do you think he might not then be allowed to

* The Most Rev. Dr. Challoner's "Catholic Christian Instructed," pp. 92, 93.

join in prayer with those of another communion, by way of supplying this defect?'

"'No, certainly. It is a misfortune, and a great misfortune, to be kept, like David when he was persecuted by Saul, at a distance from the temple [tabernacle] of God, and its sacred mysteries; but it would be *a crime to join one's self upon that account with an heretical or schismatic congregation, whose worship God rejects as sacrilegious and impious.*'

"O, now I see," cried Luella, "why you did not attend our Sunday-schools when a boy. You certainly had a good reason for it then."

"But this was not all I was taught. I was also urged to do all in my power, making use of every possible means, peacefully if I could, forcefully if I must, to convert Protestants to my faith, and thus aid in the overthrow of the most abominable and damnable heresy ever introduced into our world. I was taught that as Satan plotted and accomplished the fall of the first man, so Protestantism was a plotting to overthrow the second Adam, even Christ. This teaching was so often repeated, and with such religious emphasis, that it became interwoven into the very texture of my mental and moral being, giving peculiar colouring and potency to every thought and feeling, and controlling with more or less certainty all my actions. 'It is in the nature of man to be credulous,' says an eminent French author. 'This credulity is necessary to our conservation and development during infancy. We then receive for true, without examination, without study, opinions which cast deep roots into our minds, and which, later in life, rule us as with a tyrant's hand.' I have found it even so in my own experience.

"However, as I grew up to the age when one begins to observe the manners of mankind, I was greatly puzzled to find that the morality of my Protestant neighbours was far superior to my own and that of my people. They excelled us in acts of charity, were better educated, more refined, industrious, and sober. O what splendid Christians, I often thought—meaning of course, Roman Catholics—they would be if they only possessed the light I felt sure I had, and were members of the true Church like myself!"

"Little did you realize, even at that time," said Aunt Melie, "that the average morality of Protestants in the United States—though it is not by any means what it should be—who make no pretensions to religion, to say nothing of those who do, is superior to that of the Papists."

"But I was sure of this, that the morality of Roman Catholics in this country reaches a standard of excellence unattained and unknown in purely Roman Catholic countries."

4

"Your talk," said Luella, "reminds me of some conversation I heard in the street-cars a few days ago. One lady remarked to another, 'Have you observed the signs on the lager beer and liquor saloons and other low groggeries, which are so numerous in this city?' 'Most certainly,' replied her friend; 'and I notice that nearly every one bears a foreign name, which indicates the *religion* to which the keeper probably belongs.'"

"And yet, Luella, just look a moment at the lesson I received, in common with all Romanists of this country, on this subject. In a popular prayer-book, which is used by nearly all the people, being approved by Archbishop John Hughes, of New York, entitled 'The Way to Heaven,' we find the following instruction and prayer on page 14:—

"'By a rescript, dated 5th September, 1852, our Holy Father, Pius IX., at the instance of the National Council of Baltimore, sanctions by the grant of indulgences the institution of a society whose members shall especially pray for the conversion of all who are out of the communion of the Church in the United States.'

"'A plenary indulgence, on receiving the Easter communion, to all the members who shall daily recite, in any language, the following prayer;—

"Almighty and Eternal God, who savest all, and

wilt have none to perish, have regard to those souls who are led astray by the deceits of the devil, that, rejecting all error, the hearts of those who err may be converted, and may return to the unity of the truth, through Christ our Lord. *Amen.*"'

"Now you see that not only is the prayer taught, but this work is considered by the Pope to be of such importance, that the heavy premium of plenary indulgence—the highest ever granted—is offered to every true Romanist who repeats this brief prayer for the conversion of Protestants."

While we were thus discoursing, Johnnie had taken down the files of our daily morning paper and, interrupting us, he said, "Well, here is more light—perhaps you will say *darkness*—on the subject you are discussing. According to these facts, I think they had better get up societies to pray for the conversion of their *own* people. Just hear me read the returns from our police court."

He then read a lengthy list of arrests, presenting an unbroken array of foreign names, and remarked:—

"There, this is one day's *courting* at our police head-quarters." Turning to another and another day's account he continued for some time reading similar names in the same category, until his mother interrupted him by saying,

" That will do, I think, Johnnie ; for you might read till night and there would be no relieving of the dark picture. And it is all the darker when we consider that these are the police records of a city many of whose police, and at least one of its justices, are Roman Catholics."

" These names, though nearly all foreign, as is evident," I remarked, " may not all be the names of Romanists."

" Very true; perhaps a few are not; but as we are not personally acquainted with those individuals," replied Mrs. Beaudry, " I suppose we must draw our conclusions, guided by the positive knowledge we have of people in our own neighbourhood, and by what we learn from the criminal reports of the day—reports from penitentiaries, jails, prisons, etc. These things are truly appalling."

" My early difficulties with regard to morals, however, were not as great as when I discovered that our Protestant neighbours were not only so benevolent that Roman Catholic beggars or paupers would go to them for alms rather than to their wealthy co-religionists, or even to our priests, who always lived in the midst of abuudance, but that these ' heretics,' as we called them, were also strictly religious. Mingling among them, as we were compelled to do, I found, to my surprise. that many of them never partook of their meals without invoking God's blessing upon themselves and the food before them. Morning and evening their family circles joined in reading the Bible, also in singing hymns of praise, and in prayer—a very pious practice, which I seldom witnessed among Roman Catholics. The hours of the Sabbath were observed very sacedly, mostly in reading religious books and periodicals, and in attending public worship in churches which I found in every village and hamlet. The contrast between this state of things in Vermont and the noise and dissipation which marked the Sabbath in Lower Canada, just across the line, made a deep impression on my mind, especially as nothing but the different religions taught in these places could adequately account for these different results."

"Give us, please, some idea of the way people kept the Sabbath in Canada?" remarked Johnnie.

"The Sabbath there was a grand holiday. Rum taverns and saloons—kept in many instances, by leading members of the Church—were open all day long and thoroughly patronized, except during the hours of mass (the morning service) and vespers. Between these services, in the park right in front of the church, men and boys, and not unfrequently girls, all members of the Church, played marbles, tops, and ball, while fine horses were paraded about the

streets to advertise their beauty and speed.
You will scarcely believe me when I tell you,
that an auctioneer by the name of Demers, himself a trustee of the church, whose sons were my
school-mates, immediately after mass, mounted
a block erected for the purpose not more than
twenty feet from the church door, and, after
making several announcements of cattle strayed
away or articles found, etc., held an auction sale,
at least one day in the year, of garden seeds,
braids of flax, skeins of thread or knitting yarn,
vegetables, and live stock.   The proceeds of the
sale were turned over to the priest for prayers
and masses for the dead.   This was always preceded by a collection in church for the same
purpose.   I have seen many a cackling hen and
squealing pig sold in that way."

   "What! on the Sabbath?" exclaimed Johnnie.

   "If not on the Sabbath it was on a 'holy day
of obligation,' which they consider as sacred, and
always after high mass.   But you must remember that this was about thirty years ago, when
people in those parts were much more ignorant
than now.   These announcements from the
auction-block, made every Sabbath, were the
only means people had of advertising, for there
were probably not a half-dozen newspapers
taken in the town; and if a written notice had

been posted in a most conspicuous place in the village, not more than one person out of a hundred could have read it. Time, with increasing light, has well-nigh obliterated the traces of such disgraceful scenes in nearly all parts of that land; they continue, however, in some places."

"But what were the *private* habits of the people?" asked Luella.

"Every house in the village had its pack of cards, and card-playing and dancing, with more or less liquor-drinking, were going on in every direction."

"And did you play cards with the rest?" she inquired feelingly.

"I blush to confess it. I have often shuddered when I have thought how near I came to a gambler's life and a gambler's ruin. You will not wonder, however, when I tell you how I was taught and what examples were set before me My father took as much pains in teaching us the figures of the dance and the games at cards as my mother did in teaching us to pray. However, she did not object to the fun herself, because this amusement was universal. And as we kept a small bakery with a restaurant attached—though we sold no liquor—this state of things brought us no small gain, especially on the Sabbath. Our revenue was greatest in the season of apples, for then our house would be crowded all day long with those who bought our apples, and then gambled at cards, generally in a game called *Loo.* As I was an expert at the game, I would often win the customers' apples, and keep them buying more. So this sort of *brigandage* would go on throughout the blessed day, from morning till late at night, except during religious services, for these were always strictly and devotionally attended at the sound of the bell, and the greater our pleasures and sins at home the more earnest would be our prayers at church. And then after vespers, or afternoon service of song, father and mother would repair to the priest's house, or 'presbytery,' as it was called, and spend the remainder of the day in playing cards with the priest."

"Is it possible? What! with a priest professing to be one of the *apostles* of our Lord Jesus Christ?" ejaculated Luella.

"Yes, certainly; and yet he was one of the most devoted priests when performing the functions of his sacerdotal office that I ever saw. His name was Jean Baptiste Brouillette. He was finally selected for his great devotion as a missionary to the Indians in Oregon, where he taught the red man the poinciples of his religion."

"But what would grandfather and grandmother say to you when they returned home from these ministerial games?"

"O, they would tell us of the splendid times they had; how the jovial priest, with his tricks and cheatings with the cards—all in sport, of course—would keep the whole company for hours in an uproar of laughter. Sometimes the presbytery would be quite full. Now, I assure you that at times, young as I was, this state of things strangely puzzled my brain. The change perceptible on going from Vermont only a few miles into Canada, it seems to me, must have been much as when Christ and the favoured three descended from the Mount of Transfiguration into the valley of unbelief and demoniac possessions."

"Jesus said, 'Judge the tree by its fruit,'" remarked Mrs. Beaudry, "Why did you not apply the wholesome rule?"

"The application of this test was often urged upon my mind, but I regarded it as a temptation. I endeavoured to reason myself into the belief that this striking contrast between Protestant and Romish manners might be traced to *natural* causes mainly, such as inherited tendencies, and the different influence of soil, climate, and society amid which one is born and educated. And yet all this failed to satisfy me, and for several years the subject remained as a knotty puzzle or profound mystery."

"But," interrupted Aunt Melie, "with such

convictions in your mind, and such facts before your face, what could keep you so long in the bosom of the Church ? "

" Ah, I presume I was detained by the same powerful influences which have for centuries kept thousands of my fellow-religionists."

" This is a great puzzle to my own mind, father," said Luella, " and if you can, I wish you would explain it."

" Your request involves the whole subject of the *peculiar power or influence of the Roman Catholic Church over her members.* To present this subject fully would take more time than remains to us this afternoon. But you see that the storm increases, and is becoming so fearful that it is not probable there will be any service at the church to-night. In that event we will meet again about eight o'clock, and I will try to answer your inquiry."

Our gathering was broken up without formality, and I was left alone in my room to spend a few moments in meditation and prayer, until the sound of the tea-bell should summon me below.

IV.

THE CHURCH'S PILLARS OF STRENGTH—NORA INTER-
ESTED — LIMBUS INFANTUM — DON PIO MORTARA—
VESTMENTS AND ORNAMENTS—FETE DIEU—PURE DE-
VOTION.

And power was given him over all kindreds, and tongues, and
nations.—*Revelation.*

THERE was no cessation in the storm; it
had rather increased. During the evening the wind veered. The cold was
growing more and more intense. The
clouds lowered darkly, and prematurely
hid the day, while they poured their watery
contents down in sweeping floods. From their
angry bosoms they belched forth, Vesuvius-like,
their fiery breath, hoarsely muttering defiance
to the darkening night. The scene reminded
me of those lines of Thomson : —

" From cloud to cloud the rending lightnings rage ;
  Till, in the furious elemental war
  Dissolved, the whole precipitated mass
  Unbroken floods and solid torrents pour."

About the time of service I ventured out into
the dark, deserted streets, to ascertain whether

there was any probability of a meeting. But the sexton had not opened the church door, and the storm beat mournfully upon the darkened windows, admonishing me to hasten my return home. A few minutes before the appointed time we were again in my study. The baby's cradle was brought up, and he was snugly put to sleep.

An interesting episode must here be related. By this time Nora had become strangely interested in our study meetings. During the week the children had given her the substance of our first interview, and she was greatly pleased with the candour and Christian charity with which the whole subject had been treated. And then, drawn either by her natural curiosity or influenced by the Holy Spirit of God, she had so adroitly managed the doors leading from the study to her room, on the same floor, that, unobserved by us she overheard nearly all the conversation of the afternoon, gliding softly downstairs only just in time to prepare our evening meal.*

A few minutes before the evening gathering

---

* We do not wish to be understood as justifying Nora's plan for eavesdropping—a censurable practice, too common with some children and servants. But in this case the evil was overruled for good. This once was Nora's only offence, for which we freely forgave her.

she besought the children to intercede with me that I would permit her to come in with us. Of course my consent was readily granted, for it was just what I desired, though I had not expected that she would become interested in the matter so soon. At first, not knowing how much she knew of our former talks, I was half inclined to regard her request as a joke, or to think that a superstitious dread of being alone in any room of the house during so terrific a storm, especially in the night, led her to this desire. But I soon ascertained that she was in earnest, and that already a deep longing to know the saving truth of God's word was kindled within her. So when the children came in, they brought Nora with them.

As Luella came in holding Nora by the hand, she sat down by her side. As soon as the room became quiet, she turned to her and said:

"Nora, perhaps you, as well as father can tell me what I am especially anxious to know just now."

Nora hung her head a moment, as if abashed or a little puzzled, and then replied, "That depends on what you want to know. I'll tell you if I can."

"Well, can you tell me what is the chief corner-stone, or the principal pillar of strength, in your Church?"

She hesitated for some moments as if in deep study, and then slowly said, "I—suppose,—child,—it is—her infallibility;" but seeming not to be fully satisfied herself with the answer, she added, "Wait a bit, dear; I think it is rather *her great attention to children.*"

"Nora has struck the key-note," I said; "you may depend upon that. In this matter, however, Roman Catholics follow illustrious examples—even that of the old Jewish Church, and of Christ, who, setting a child in the midst of His Disciples, said, 'Of such is my kingdom, and all men must become like this child to enter therein.'"

"But," said Aunt Melie, "does the Romish Church present the same motives, and does she act with the same spirit?"

"Let us examine," I said. "In order to reap as great a harvest here as possible, she strenuously teaches that no child dying unbaptized can possibly enter heaven, but must forever be detained in a mournful region which she calls '*limbus infantum.*' She does not permit unbaptized children to be buried with others, but puts them by themselves in a sort of potter's field."

"There, I thought there was something fundamentally wrong," added Aunt Melie, "in her teaching here. Why, nothing is plainer than that the covenant which God made with our father Abraham included himself and children, and that all received circumcision as a *seal of their acceptance with God*, and not to make them acceptable. So now children should be baptized, *because they already belong to Christ* and are of his kingdom, but not to make them such. Baptism can in no case create the union of a soul to Christ; it only recognizes and seals it."

"You have planted your banner on scriptural ground, I am sure," I replied. "But the Roman Catholic Church urges the reverse of this. Thus she seeks to baptize not only the children of families where both parents are Romanists, but also where only one of them is in the faith, and not unfrequently she reaches the children of those who are wholly non-Roman.* To accomplish this, notwithstanding the sacredness which the Church attaches to the sacraments, she teaches that baptism may be administered by any person, in what she calls 'cases of necessity.'† This can be done by a heretic even, or

---

* A Romish priest under oath not long since made the following statement : "I believe I have divine authority to secure Protestant children from their Protestant mothers and *make* them Catholics. I deny the right of a Protestant minister to do the same."

† Dr. Challoner's "Catholic Instructed," p. 24. "Petit Catechisme," p. 51.

by an ignorant servant-boy or girl, as well as by a bishop."

So saying, the children turned their eyes towards Nora, who, as I waited a moment, hoping she might say something, remarked, " All this is true, but I wouldn't for the life of me that Protestants generally should know it."

" Why not, if it be true ? " quickly asked Luella.

" Why, don't you see that many of us poor servant-girls would be sure to lose our places ? for Protestants wouldn't have us in their families if they knew these things, though we only do what we are ordered to do by the Church. And, faith, I have known of several children of Protestant families brought into our Church in this very way, when nobody but the priest and myself, or some friend of mine, knew anything about it, until it was too late for them." Here she stopped abruptly, became nervous under the excited gaze of the children, and, indeed, of the rest of the company, and, as a fearful peal of thunder shook the house, crossed herself and exclaimed, " Ah, me ! may the holy Virgin Mary and St. Honora, my patron saint, protect me ! for I didn't mean to turn informer on our good priests, much less on myself. O, what would I give if I had never said a word about it ! "

" Now, Nora." I mildly remarked, hoping to

remove her embarrassment, "you need not be
so troubled about what you have said, for, in
the first place, the general practice of your
Church in this direction was well known to me
before you spoke ; and, in the second place, you
ought not to be afraid to tell the truth at any
time. It is already a matter of history that in 1858
a boy, seven years old, named Edgar Mortara, the
son of a Jew at Bologna, then in the Pontifical
States, was forcibly taken from his parents and
placed in a Papal school at Rome, where he subsequently became a monk in one of the principal
convents, and was known as Don Pio Mortara.
The ground on which he was taken was his
alleged baptism, when an infant and dangerously
sick, by a servant-girl in his father's family.*
In all these cases the little *protégés* are looked
after with untiring zeal, and, if possible, brought
within the scope of the Church's power.   A
child can be taught to believe anything.   Faith,
in the human breast, is as spontaneous and
natural as is breathing to the lungs, and no one
ever begins to doubt or question until he is conscious of having been deceived."

"Mr. Spurgeon recently said," added Mrs.
Beaudry, "'I have, during the past year,
received forty or fifty children into Church-

---

* Rev. S. W. Barnum's "Romanism As It Is," p. 648.

membership. Among those I have had at any
time to exclude from Church-fellowship, out of
a Church of twenty-seven hundred members, I
never had to exclude a single one who was
received while yet a child.' Even so the Church
must learn that if she would subdue the world
to Christ she must bring her children to her
altars in very infancy, and in the family train
them thoroughly for this holy war."

At this point I assured Nora that nothing she
had confessed should be permitted, at least if I
could prevent it, to return upon her to her
injury. Meanwhile Luella, in sympathy, had
thrown her arms around the agitated girl, drawing her close to her side, so as to lean her head
upon her shoulder. Quietness having been fully
restored, Johnnie remarked:

"But this does not explain all the power of
the Church, does it?"

"O, no. Her power, especially over children
and the masses, is found also in *her method of
object-teaching, or use of symbols, which appeal
to the external senses.* In this regard she
greatly resembles the Jewish Church. The
artist is doing vastly more in the Church than
the priest. The elaborate paintings on the walls
of the churches; the gorgeous display of ornaments on the high altars; the splendid crucifixes
and ponderous statues; the ever-burning lamps

and tapers; the swinging and smoking censers; oratorios performed in the highest style of the musical art on pealing organs; the gaudy attire of officiating priests and acolytes, or attendants, with the varied and theatrical changes of the services, are the chief attractions, both gravitating and cohesive, of the Church. Strip her of these, and what would remain? Preaching is but a small item in the services of the Romish Church, and often there is no preaching at all. The people are not generally instructed, but amused.

"No pains are spared to vary the above attractions to suit them to the changing seasons and to all occasions. For instance, during Lent the churches are draped in mourning, and the general services are more solemn than usual, culminating in the most funereal solemnities during Passion Week. The altars are then stripped of their ornaments, the crucifixes and altar-pieces are draped or covered, the windows are darkened, and the lamps so arranged as to shed the most melancholy light throughout the edifices. On Wednesday, Thursday, and Friday evenings are celebrated the *tenebræ* offices, so called from the Latin word for darkness, because toward the end of the service all the lights are extinguished, in memory of the darkness which covered all the earth while Christ was hanging on the cross; and at the close of the offices on Friday night, a noise is made by the congregation's clapping of hands, or striking the bench before them, to represent the earthquake and rending of rocks, which happened at the moment when our Lord expired. This rite is not performed in all places, but usually in metropolitan churches or cathedrals.

"From the evening of Good Friday a cenotaph, or memorial tomb of Christ, is erected near the altar, at which, night and day, two boys belonging to the choir, and dressed in white robes in imitation of the angels, watch while they read and repeat solemn prayers. I have spent many hours in these mournful vigils, hoping thereby to gain some great indulgence from the Lord. We were relieved by others every hour. During this time a large crucifix, intended to represent the dead Saviour, is exposed in the church, at a point convenient of access, and multitudes of people visit it, and kiss it. These occasions left a deep impression upon my sympathetic nature. This service continues until early Easter morning, at the time it is supposed Christ rose from the tomb, when every vestige of mourning is removed, and the greatest gaiety and jubilation are introduced into every sight and sound. During the month of May, which is especially consecrated to the worship of the Virgin Mary, there is the greatest display of flowers in the

churches, and the services are of the most joyfu
kind."

"These things are so," said Nora; "I have
often seen them."

"Certainly; 'that which I have seen and
heard declare I unto you.' And I have still more
to tell you. The vestments of the priests officiating at masses are peculiarly attractive. They
are the amice, the alb, the girdle, the maniple,
the stole, and the chasuble. All these are taste-
fully and gaudily made and trimmed. 'In these
vestments,' says Rev. Dr. Challoner,* 'the
Church makes use of five colours—the *white*, on
the feast of our Lord, of the blessed Virgin, of
the angels, and of the saints that were not
martyrs; the *red*, on the feast of Pentecost, on
the invention (discovery) and exaltation of the
cross, and of the apostles and martyrs; the
green, on the greatest part of Sundays; the
violet, in the penitential times of Advent and
Lent, and upon vigils and Ember days; and the
black, upon Good Friday and the masses for the
dead.'

"In addition to these symbols, I ought to
mention those employed in Roman Catholic
countries like Lower Canada. Along most of
the thoroughfares the traveller is surprised to

* "The Catholic Instructed," p. 82.

find every few miles a cross about twenty feet high, beautified with modern art, before which the devout remove their hats as they pass, and make the sign of the cross upon their breasts, and around whose base the ground is beaten hard and smooth by the knees of the peasants and villagers who come there at eventide, at some seasons of the year, to offer their devotions. The highest mountains and hills are also adorned with crosses, which the faithful frequently visit in holy pilgrimages. Nearly every house, barn, and even outhouse is surmounted by a cross, many of the citizens preferring them to light-ning-rods, and using them for the same pur-pose.

"Previous to their erection, those large public crosses are carried about the streets in pompous and solemn processions, while music, both vocal and intrumental, rends the air, and brilliant flags and banners float over the assembled multitudes. Frequently flowers in great profusion are strewn along the way for the officiating bishop or priest to walk upon. I have gathered many a basket of flowers from the fields for these occasions, thinking that God would greatly bless me for the deed. Public processions take place several days in the year, the grandest occuring on what they call the feast of *Corpus Christi*—the body of Christ. At this procession, the priest, arrayed in the most gorgeous robes, carries a consecrated wafer, which is believed now to be the real body of Christ, in a golden pyx or box, and walks under a beautiful silken canopy borne by four men. He is preceded by one man with the flowers and another with a smoking censer, who walk backward so as to face the priest, casting the flowers and swinging the censer, as they keep time with the music and the moving throng. Now, when you consider that all these symbols and celebrations are regarded as religious services and holy sacrifices, acceptable to God and beneficial to souls here and hereafter, you will not wonder that children and thousands of adults, especially women, are drawn to the Church by them."

"O, how earnest and devoted Roman Catholics must be to do all these things," said Luella.

"But in what part of the Bible do you find that God's people are directed or instructed to worship him in any such way?" asked Aunt Melie.

"We find it in our prayer-books, ma'am," said Nora; "and can we do too much for God?"

"No, indeed," answered Mrs. Beaudry, "when we are guided by his blessed Spirit and word. But there is a zeal which is not according to knowledge, and which is injurious. Jesus has taught us that God is a spirit, and that true worshippers must worship the Father in spirit

and in truth—that is, in sincerity, under the
guidance of the Holy Spirit, and in accordance
with his revealed truth. All our services should
be simple, and thus adapted to all classes of
people—the poor, the ignorant, the sick. They
ought to be the natural outgushings of pure
hearts, spontaneous as the light which emanates
from the sun, silent yet glorious ; or as the water
which flows clear and cool from bubbling springs,
to refresh the flowers that grow along the banks
of the brooklet, and to make the meadows green.
It is, above all things, a pure heart that Jesus
wants ; a heart in which He may dwell, and
make it the temple of the Holy Spirit. All that
we can do with our hands or feet is nothing in
comparison with the heart's pure adoration and
love, and that service of 'a quiet and peaceable
life' which is rendered 'in all godliness and
honesty'—a life which seeks to know and then
to do the will of God."

"You speak beautifully, ma'am; I wish 1
could speak as well. O how long I have desired
to have such a pure heart as you speak of—a
heart that would love and praise God as naturally as flowers exhale their sweet odours, or
even such a one as I think yours must be, which
keeps you calm and gentle in the midst of care
and provocation, and gives you such a happy,
even temper."

Almost blushing under such an unexpected sally of praise, Mrs. Beaudry responded: "Why, Nora, you surprise me! I would advise you not to take me, or any other creature for your model, but take Jesus, who is our only Saviour, and the perfect pattern of his people. He will grant you just such a heart and life as you desire, if you seek it with a right spirit."

Here looking at my watch I found that it was about our usual time for retiring. So interrupting this interesting train of remarks—though the subject we had been discussing was not exhausted—I suggested that we must terminate our interview. "But let us first kneel down to offer our evening prayer,. and ask our heavenly Father for his illumination and guidance."

This season of devotion was peculiarly refreshing, and at its close we repeated in concert, as we always do, the following little prayer:

> "And now we lay us down to sleep,
> We pray the Lord our souls to keep;
> And should we die before we wake,
> We pray the Lord our souls to take.
> And this we ask for Jesus' sake. Amen."

Then the children, as is their habit after all our family devotions, came each in turn for their kiss, before I rose from my knees; and when

Mary had embraced me she *naively* said, while yet the storm was howling terribly without:

"Father, the Lord can keep us, can't He, although the night is so dark and stormy?"

"O, yes my child; He keeps even the little birds and insects to-night, so that not one of them can suffer or fall without His notice. I can trust you in the care of Him to 'whom the darkness and the light are both alike.' And now good-night."

As they withdrew through the hall, I heard Luella repeating to the others a few lines of a favourite hymn from the pen of Henry Kirke White:

"Ye winds of night, your force combine;
  Without His high behest,
Ye shall not, in the mountain pine,
  Disturb the sparrow's rest.

"His voice sublime is heard afar;
  In distant peals it dies;
He yokes the whirlwind to His car,
  And sweeps the howling skies."

V.

*And he causeth all, both small and great, rich and poor, free and bond,
to receive a mark in their right hand, or in their foreheads.—Apocalypse.*

THE week had glided by without any
special incident, save that a deepening
religious feeling was observable in all,
particularly in Nora, who seemed to hail
the seasons of family prayer with much
more than her former interest. When she first
came to live with us she appeared even loth to
hear us read the Bible lessons, but now she
gladly participated with us in the pleasing
exercise; and when the Sabbath afternoon came,
instead of going to vespers, as she used to do,
she was one of the first to repair to my study to
arrange things for our meeting there.

On assembling this time I told them that I
had already described two of the leading ele-

ments of power in the Church, answering to the two leading senses in the human body, namely, seeing and hearing, for the eye is delighted to behold the symbols with which the Church is filled, and the ear is charmed in listening to her instruments of music and cultured voices; but the third element of strength answers very nearly to feeling. It is this: *The Church ingeniously furnishes to every one of her members, old and young, good, bad, and indifferent, something considered religious to do or bear in nearly all her services, and every day of life.*

"What does she give children to do?" asked Johnnie, who is always ready to act as well as to think. "Does she let them sing?"

"Most certainly; their choirs are largely made up of children, and thus become the more attractive. But then this is not all they let the children do. When a large cross was consecrated and erected at Henryville, I carried a beautiful crucifix which my mother had purchased for me; and there was scarcely a child or adult but had either a crucifix, or a medal, or a prayer-book, or a string of rosary beads, or a scapular."

"What do you mean by this last?" again inquired Johnnie.

"I shall have to tell you some other time, at least if you can wait."

"Certainly; but what did you do with those things there?"

"When the bishop sprinkled the great cross with holy water, and afterward the multitudes, these crucifixes and other things were held out so as to receive at least a drop of the water, after which they were said to be endowed with great spiritual, and even miraculous, power. For instance, if any one was taken suddenly and dangerously ill, the crucifix would be laid on his breast until the parish priest arrived to administer what they call the 'sacrament of extreme unction.' The crucifix was supposed to have power to prolong the life of the invalid, at least until the priest's arrival.

"My mother used to talk to us for hours about the miracles performed by these and other sacred relics. Our prayer-books and books of instruction were also full of these accounts. The crucifix I carried on the day referred to was sacredly preserved in the family for at least a score of years, and was always resorted to in hours of trouble and danger."

"But, father, are these the only occasions in which every one can do something which is considered especially pious?" asked Luella.

"No, indeed. At least once a year, on Maundy-Thursday of Passion Week (the last week of Lent), the same day on which the Pope and bishops consecrate the holy *chrism,* or oil of olives and balm of Gilead, as they say it is, a large tub or hogshead of pure water is brought into the church."

"O how funny!" exclaimed Mary. "Do they bring it there to swim in, father ? "

"Why no, my child.   It is brought there to be made into *holy water.*"

"I should like to know how that is done," observed Luella.

"I will try to tell you. The priest and his attendants gather around the tub or vessel, sing Latin hymns, and repeat prayers and litanies ; then he casts a little salt, previously exorcised by solemn ceremony, into the water, saying, ' I exorcise thee, O creature of water, in the name of God the Father Almighty, and in the name of Jesus Christ His Son our Lord, and in the virtue of the Holy Ghost, that Thou mayest by this exorcism have power to chase away all the power of the enemy ; that thou mayest be enabled to cast him out and put him to flight, with all his apostate angels, by the virtue of the same Jesus Christ our Lord, who is to come to judge the living and the dead, and the world by fire.   Amen.' " *

"But what do they mean by the word *exorcism ?* "

* Dr Challoner's "Catholic Instructed," p. 203.

" I will give you the definition of the Church :
' The rites and prayers instituted by the Church
for casting out devils, or restraining them from
hurting persons, disquieting places, or abusing
any of God's creatures to our harm.' When the
above prayers have been duly repeated, the
water is pronounced holy."

"What do they do with this water ?" inquired
Johnnie.

"The uses are various. Some is kept in a font
by the church door for every one who enters
or retires to sprinkle himself with ; the altar
and the people are sprinkled with it at the
beginning of mass ; it is sprinkled upon the
coffins and graves of the dead ; on the ashes used
on Ash-Wednesday ; on the ring used at marriage ceremonies, and on persons consecrated to
any special religious purpose. It is also employed
in the baptism of persons and things considered
sacred, such as church bells, candles or tapers
for the altar, or to burn by the side of the
dead ; and the sick-room is usually well fur-
nished with it.

" On the days when it is made, every family,
and sometimes every member of the family,
brings a bottle or vial, which is filled with the
consecrated element ; and every home is thus
supplied. It is recommended by the authorities,
as you might infer from the prayer of consecra-

tion, as being very sacred, and securing God's protection and blessing upon those who use it; and, like the crucifixes and other things mentioned before, it is believed to have power to work miracles, particularly upon those occasions when it is used against magical enchantments and the power of the devil." *

"O it is only the ignorant and superstitious who believe in such trinkets," said Nora, who had been quiet for some time, but now felt herself called out to vindicate her Church.

"You forget, I fear, Nora, that these 'trinkets,' as you style them, are things solemnly consecrated by bishops and priests who teach the people in their Catechisms that they are important, and should be used in their devotions. It is rather the unbelieving who refuse to accept or use them."

"You are right, I must confess," she replied; "I know it, though I earnestly wish it were otherwise."

"On Palm Sunday," I continued "the first day of Passion Week, there is another great procession, the streets having been previously adorned with evergreens. Bishop Fenwick tells us that this is in honor of our Lord's triumphant entry into Jerusalem, and is so called from the

* Rt. Rev. Bp. Fenwick's "Catholic Catechism," p. 82.

palm branches strewed under his feet by the Hebrew children. On this day the Church blesses palms, that is, sprinkles them with holy water, and makes a solemn procession, in memory of the triumph of our Saviour, the people bearing palm branches. Thus, besides participating in the procession, every one, old and young, carries a twig of spruce, hemlock, pine, or palm, as a part of the religious ceremony. After the sprig is sprinkled, it is taken home and carefully preserved."

"But what good does it do?" inquired Johnnie.

"The people are taught that it is a sure protection from injury by the elements as well as from the attacks of Satan. I well recollect when, at the beginning of such a storm as prevailed last Sabbath, my mother would say to us, '*Apportez le rameau*'—bring the branch; and then plucking the leaflets she would put them into our hair, and piously sprinkle us with holy water; and then at every gleam of lightning we made the sign of the cross upon ourselves, and felt perfectly secure. Many Roman Catholics believe that these things will often divert storms from their destined course, and also quench the violence of fire."

"How is it, then," inquired Johnnie, " that Romish countries, even more, I think, than

6

Protestant, are so frequently visited with dreadful storms, hurricanes, and earthquakes; and that fires are so prevalent in Roman Catholic cities, often burning their churches and schools, as was the case in Montreal, July 8th and 9th, 1852, as I remember reading? The destruction was terrible, and mostly of Roman Catholic property."

"Look right at home," added Luella. "You remember how lightning struck one of the turrets of St. Joseph's Church, and damaged the building, while no other church was touched. And also in the terrible calamity that laid Chicago in ashes, but a short time ago, Romish Churches and convents formed no barrier to the tide of fire which swept them away." Then turning to Nora, she said, " And what do *you* think about these facts, which you know as well as the rest of us?"

"Like most children," answered Nora, appearing a little provoked, "you ask more questions than *anybody* can answer. At the same time, I am led to suspect that there is a great deal of hollow pretence in the Church."

"Be this as it may," I interrupted, "you can see what power these teachings exercise over the people, as they constantly participate in such services at home and at church. This was espe-

cially the case with our family. My parents
were not only prominent and devoted members
of the Church, but my father was for many
years a leading singer in the choir, and also
belonged to the board of 'syndics,' or officers of
the Church. To complete our attachment, your
Uncle Charles and myself were put into the
choir—made *enfants de chœur*, or altar-boys, as
we were called—where we not only sang, but
frequently took our turns in waiting on the
priest during mass and vespers. We were
dressed in long flowing gowns ; and if you will
look at the pictures in Bishop Fenwick's Catechism, beginning at page 92, you will see what
we mainly had to do. We engaged in those
ceremonies with great devotion. It required
long and tedious training to learn the Latin
service, with its many responses, not a word of
which we understood ; and also to know at
what time to raise the trail of the priest's
chasuble ; to ring a little bell ; to bow here and
go their ; to give the priest his portion of wine ;
then water to wash his fingers in imitation of
Pilate, and to perform our part in the varying
scenes of this long religious drama. But having
learned these things thoroughly, we were the
more punctual in our attendance at church, for
whole months together going every day. Low

mass, as it is called, is celebrated every morning of week days, throughout the year, except on Good Friday, and high mass on Sundays. Low mass is sometimes celebrated on Sunday also. The latter is simply spoken, and sometimes so rapidly, especially by some priests, that you can distinguish only a continuous buzz; but the former is sung or chanted by the priest and the whole choir in very grand style."

"I would certainly like to attend the services you have been describing," said Luella. "Won't you take me to them some time?"

"And won't you take *me* too?" asked Johnnie.

"And me too, father?" followed Mary.

"Yes, children, at the very first opportunity you shall see for yourselves at least some of the things I have attempted to describe; and if I can't go with you, perhaps Nora will be willing to go in my place."

"I don't know about that," replied Nora, with a peculiar twinkle in her eyes. "Your talk makes me feel almost ashamed of the whole thing; and then if I should take the children, I'm a little afraid they might ask me too many questions."

"Never mind now; we'll try to make this all right somehow." Having called their attention from this thing, I said,

"I want to mention now another element of

power in the Church, namely, *the mystery with which she invests every religious subject."*

"Is it not true," asked Nora, "that religion is a very mysterious thing?"

"I admit that in revelation, as in nature, there are many mysteries; but there are also many things which can be well known and understood. For instance, who can solve the mystery of nutrition even? Who can tell us how food taken into the stomach becomes blood, bones, nerves, muscles, tissues, nails, hair, etc.? Yet who does not know and cannot tell us when his hunger is satisfied and his body strengthened by nourishment? Thus the known and the unknown go hand in hand all the way through the operations of nature. The same is true in revelation, showing the God of the one to be the God of the other also. But the Romish Church makes no such distinction as nature and revelation indicate. She robes *every* phase of religion in profound mystery, forgetting that while it is true that we cannot know *everything* about anything, it is equally true that we may positively know *something* about everything. Hence she says, 'Away with your reason when you come into the temple of God!' To add force to this teaching, she worships in an unknown tongue; she complicates her system with numerous classes of priests and 'religious,' male and female, each with their strange and mystic garb, making them appear like different orders of beings from the common people ; and when science, however strongly entrenched, contradicts her theories, she blindly rejects the known truth for her favourite mysteries. Recall the history of Galileo and hundreds of others. But God addresses man thus, ' Come now, and let us reason together.' There must, therefore, be *some* religious subjects which the reason can grapple with and ought to solve. ' Prove all things,' says Paul, ' hold fast that which is good.'"

" Our priests tell us that we must believe and receive all that *they* teach us without asking any questions for conscience' sake," remarked Nora, " because they say, he who questions shows doubts, and the Scriptures declare that ' he that doubteth is damned. "'

" This is a favourite text of theirs, I know, and their comment upon it is drawn from the Saviour's own words to doubting Thomas, ' Blessed are they that have not seen and yet have believed.' Bishop Fenwick, in his Catechism, is heard asking the children of his diocese, (Boston, Mass.)—

"' How shall we know the things which we are to believe ?'

"' *Answer.* From the Catholic Church of God, which He has established by innumerable miracles, and illustrated by the lives and deaths of innumerable saints.'

"And further on he asks again :—

"'Are we bound to obey the commandments of the Church ?'

"'Yes; because Christ has said to the pastors of his Church, He that heareth you heareth me; and he that despiseth you despiseth me.'"

"Are not all these things in the Bible?' asked Nora.

"Certainly; but we are to exercise our reason as to *what* Church has the Divine authority to command and to teach, for Christ said, 'Ye shall know them by their works, as trees are known by their fruits;' and even then we are not to receive their doctrines with a thoughtless assent, or without the closest scrutiny. Each member of the Church has a duty here, as well as his instructors; he must know these things for himself, at least as far as experimental and practical religion is concerned. Every true believer will admit that there is much mystery as to the sources or causes of redemption, yet nothing is plainer from Scripture, or more clearly exemplified in the experience of thousands of Christians, than that he who accepts pardon may *know* it, so that it becomes at last a matter of experience. Paul says, 'And without controversy great is the mystery of godliness: God was *manifest* in the flesh, justified in the Spirit, seen of angels, preached unto the Gentiles, *believed on in the world*, received up into glory.' Here we have the incarnation of Christ as a glorious mystery, but his manifestation was well known to angels and to men, challenging the admiration of the former and the faith of the latter. And Peter, writing to his brethren of Christ, says : ' Whom having not seen ye love ; in whom, though now you see him not, yet believing, ye rejoice with joy unspeakable and full of glory, receiving (now) the end of your faith, even the salvation of your souls.'. Here we see the true meaning of the text, 'Blessed are they that have not seen and yet have believed.' It is believing in Christ, and not in men."

" Why, father," said Johnnie, "your talk reminds me of telegraphing ; you know how mysterious all the operations are, but the messages are easily understood."

" The Scriptures are full of this thought," 1 replied. " The young man born blind, speaking of Christ to the Pharisees, who were questioning him about his recovery, exclaimed, ' Whether He be a sinner or no, I know not,' that is a mystery to me; ' one thing I know, that whereas I was blind, now I see.' "

"May we know it for sure?" inquired Nora, longingly.

"Yes, indeed," responded two or three voices in the room.

"Job said," I added, "'I know that my Re-deemer liveth.' Paul: 'I know whom I have believed.' John: 'We know that we have passed from death unto life.' This is the uniform and universal testimony of the word of God. But the teaching of the Roman Catholic Church upon this point has its designed effect. She seems to regard the common people as a herd of imbeciles, and by her treatment reduces many of them to mere automatons. We had a good illustration of this a few days ago. The follow-ing conversation took place between a Protestant drayman and a Romish coal-heaver :—

"'Patrick, what do you believe?'

"'B'lave, shure,' replied Patrick, 'I b'lave what the Roman Catholic Church b'laves.'

"'Well, Patrick, what does the Church believe?'

"'Shure, man, the Church b'laves what I b'lave.'

"'Now, Patrick, what do you both believe?'

"'Well, by my sowl, we both b'lave alike.'"

"This is implicit faith. Thus the Church steals away the brains of her people and stulti-fies them. She quenches in them all desire

to use their reasoning faculties on religious subjects, while she invests herself, and especially
the priesthood, with an undefined, mysterious
power which is almost omnipotent with the
masses of her people."

"If indeed the Roman Catholic Church is
wrong," said Nora thoughtfully, "how shall
poor sinners learn where to go among so many
different Protestant Churches?"·

" Your question reminds me of another great
element of power in your Church, which, as I
shall explain it, will, I trust, throw some light
upon this subject, and that is, *her boasted unity
as against Protestant sectarianism.* However,
let us not confound unity with mere conformity.
She brandishes before the nations the beautiful
Latin tongue which she employs in all her
services, endeavouring thereby to impress them
with the belief that all her people, or those who
hold to her general confession of faith, are one
in feeling, in doctrine, in practice. On the
other hand, she affirms that Protestants are
divided into numberless petty sects or denominations, as antagonistic to each other as they
are to the Roman Catholic Church, and that the
Protestant world is as much confused as was
ancient Babel. 'According to their own teaching,' she says, 'there must be an Episcopalian
God, a Presbyterian God, a Methodist God, and

a Baptist God, certainly as many deities as there
are sects ; ' and she asserts that the most charitable conclusion to be drawn is, that Protestantism is a grand religious farce, or a horrible
rebellion against God, adapted to satisfy the
caprice of vicious, designing men."

"But what are the facts in the case ?" asked
Aunt Melie.

"Here they are : that the differences among
Protestants are so slight as scarcely to be worth
mentioning ; that they generally relate to Church
government or discipline, and not to doctrines ;
and that these differences are far less than those
found in the organizations of the different
societies, confraternities, or sodalities, etc., of
monks and nuns, or ' brothers' and 'sisters,' in
the Roman Catholic Church. I mean the
Jesuits, the Sulpicians, the Dominicans, the
Franciscans, etc., etc. Our Protestant denominations may well be compared to the different
tribes of Israel, or to the different regiments of
an army, each with its peculiar badges or
insignia, its peculiar uniform and equipment,
suited to the arm of the service to which it
belongs, but all under the command of one
General, actuated by one common impulse and
motive, and accomplishing one great work. In
proof of this statement I cite the general organizations to which all evangelical denominations

belong, such as the American and Foreign
Christian Union, the American Bible Society,
the Evangelical Alliance, and the Young Men's
Christian Associations.   Here is still more convincing proof, in the fact that our religious
services are attended by members of all denominations indiscriminately; that ministers of different Churches exchange pulpit labours; and
that many of the members of some Churches
were converted at the altars of others, and *vice
versa.*"

"Furthermore, every careful reader of the
times can see that while Protestants are becoming more and more alike in their principles and
spirit, Roman Catholics, on the other hand, are becoming more and more unlike each other. Witness
the dissensions and divisions among Romanists
during the discussions, and since the procla-
mation, of the dogma of the Pope's infallibility.
This doctrine has fallen among them as a bone
of contention, though the masses had long been
trained for its reception.   This was the case also
with the doctrine of the Virgin Mary's immaculate conception.   The doctrine that the Pope is
infallible was taught me more than thirty years
ago.   I was told that the priest receives his power
from the bishop, he from the archbishop, this
from the cardinal, and the last from the Pope."

"But where does the Pope get his power

from ? " inquired Johnnie, who is always anxious
to probe things to the bottom.

" Directly from God, with whom, I was taught,
he communicated at least once a year by means
of a letter."

" O how I would like to be the Pope's post-
boy then ! " he jokingly added, causing a little
laughter.

"But now, while some countries and prelates
accept the doctrine, many reject it, notwithstanding the appeals and threats made to them ;
until at last 'the Pope hurls his dreadful
anathema at no less a scholar and Christian
than Dr. Von Dollinger, of Bavaria, whose
opposition is sustained by the leading univer-
sities and professors of his own and other lands.
Thus a party of 'Old Catholics,' as they very
correctly call themselves, is forming, which
threatens the Roman Catholic Church with
dismemberment and discomfiture, at least in
Germany."

"The sky reddens with wrath," said Aunt
Melie, "against the Pope and his party in
Europe."

" It is true," I added, " for even papalized
Italy, by a unanimity of voice and vote seldom
paralleled in the history of nations, ejects the
sovereign (?) pontiff from the throne of his
regal power, against his most solemn protests

and warnings. They persist in their course like one who tries to slough off from his vitals a deadly, putrid cancer, notwithstanding the pleadings of Roman Catholic France, for so many years the mainstay of the Pope, but now, through her own arrogance, most pitifully humbled in her unsuccessful contest with Protestant Prussia. Italy has not even heeded the prayers of Roman Catholics in America, who paraded our streets in mammoth processions, and were harangued on the subject by their leading men in their grand churches and cathedrals. There is no union of heart between different Romanized nations, but rather enmity, as, for instance, between the French and Irish in this country. A sample of this was given recently in the city of Quebec. And yet you must remember that all these schisms are occurring among a people who boast of being governed by one head, and in whose Catechisms we are told that ' the Pope is the Bishop of Rome, the first of bishops, the Successor of St. Peter, the Vicar of Jesus Christ on earth, the centre of Catholic unity, and visible Chief of the Church." *

"On the other hand, the oneness of Protestants is not derived from any centralization of power in one man or a select few, but they are drawn together by their common attachment to

* Petit Catéchisme, p. 24.

the truth of God—by the unifying influence of a pure Christianity. It is the 'unity of the Spirit in the bond of peace.' If this was not strictly true of Protestants in the distant past, it is true of them to-day ; and may it please the Lord to make it true, sooner or later, of all the nations and peoples who profess the Christian name !"

"Amen !" responded my auditors, whose interest had waxed stronger as I advanced with my argument.

At this interesting point of our discussion our door-bell was rung, and a messenger, who had come in great haste, announced that one of our Sunday-school scholars, having been taken suddenly ill, was lying apparently at the point of death, and was very anxious to see me. So, leaving my company, I hastened to relieve, as far as possible, the wants of the dying scholar. I found him very near the gates of death, but in a very happy frame of mind. He told me of his child-like trust in Jesus, who had forgiven all his sins, and thus prepared him for this last change. How heavenly was the influence of the chamber of death as we joined in singing :—

"Jesus can make a dying bed
Feel soft as downy pillows are,
While on his breast I lean my head,
And breathe my life out sweetly there."

VI.

To Whom My Sins Confess ?—Monsieur Grenier—
Agreement and Disagreement — Confessional
Described—Preparations for Confession—One
Mediator.

*If we confess our sins, He is faithful and just to forgive us our sins, and
to cleanse us from all unrighteousness.—John.*

THE week had been eventful. With the
children and their mother I had visited
St. Joseph's Roman Catholic Church,
where we spent some time in interesting
observation and study. Meanwhile we
had formed what seemed to be, especially at this
time, a providential acquaintance, under the
following circumstances. One evening I received
a letter from a ministerial brother in a neighbouring parish, which ran thus :—

"DEAR BROTHER :—Your help is very much
needed. A French Roman Catholic, a young
man of intelligence and refinement, called on me
last night to ask me some questions about his

and our religion. He says he felt well enough
till he got hold of the Bible, since which time he
has had no peace of mind. About two weeks
ago he thought he would become insane if he
did not get help. I talked and prayed with
him, and gave him Wesley's Sermons and Peck's
Rule of Faith as the best books I could think of
in my possession, and told him of you. His eye
brightened when I told him I would go with
him to see you. He is anxious to come immediately.... Yours fraternally,

"JOEL K. WAGER."

The young man's name and place of business
were given, and an answer was desired to
inform them when I would be home, with leisure
to meet them. But I was too much interested
in the case to wait for the return of mail, so I
went early the next morning and found him.
His name is Charles Willie Grenier. Though
thoroughly educated in the College of the
Jesuits in Montreal, and, up to the time of his
getting a Bible, only a few months ago, passion-
ately devoted to the Church, with an uncle in
the priesthood and all his family in the faith, I
found him grasping evangelical teaching with
wonderful eagerness, and resolved at any cost
to seek the truth as it is in Jesus. He assured
me that all the efforts of his priest to turn his

7

mind from this direction only drove him further from that Church.

Our interview was mutually agreeable, and he promised to spend a Lord's Day with me, requesting the privilege of participating with the family in our afternoon *séance* in my study as I had not failed to inform him of our arrangement. This privilege was readily granted, and when the time arrived his presence among us added much to the enthusiasm already kindled. His language, though chaste, was nevertheless considerably broken; and when he failed to express his views with sufficient clearness in English, he would politely ask the ladies to excuse him, while he took the liberty of speaking to me in his "*belle langue Française,*" as he called his vernacular. This gave fresh interest to our subjects, and introduced a novelty with which the children especially were greatly delighted. Even Nora, though at first a little shy of him, was charmed with the urbanity of his manners. After a few preliminaries, Monsieur Grenier remarked:—

"There is one thing about Protestants I am very anxious to learn (*je désire ardemment d'apprendre*), whether there is any subject in religion upon which they agree, in the main, with Roman Catholics."

"There is no lack of such subjects, I assure

you," I replied. "Here is one right at hand and familiar to us all: it is sin. I ought, perhaps, to remark at the very outset that however much men may differ in their theories, they generally agree in matters of experience. And with regard to this subject of sin, Protestants and Romanists perfectly agree:

"1st. That we are all sinners; that 'all we like sheep have gone astray,' 'for all have sinned and come short of the glory of God.' Here there is no difference between Jew and Gentile, between priest and people.

"2nd. We agree that sin is the cause of all human misery; that it separates the soul from God, and puts men at war with Him, with one another, and with themselves.

"3rd. We agree that since all sin is hateful in the sight of God, it causes the fear of death; that while 'the wages of sin is death,' the 'sting of death is sin.'

"4th. We agree that no sin can enter heaven; that the soul must be perfectly free from sin and all its stains to enter into that holy place, for 'without holiness no man shall see the Lord.'

"5th. We agree that Jesus Christ became a sin-offering for us; that he is 'the Lamb of God which taketh away the sin of the world.' In my Little Catechism the question is asked 'What did Jesus Christ accomplish on the earth?' The answer is, 'He taught men to live holily, and merited or obtained for them the grace so to do.' This we all fully hold.

" 6th. We further agree that to get rid of our sins we must confess them. This we all believe must be done with the deepest sorrow for having offended God, and with a full determination to abandon every sinful thing, and to live wholly devoted to God. On the 66th page of my 'Petit Catéchisme' is taught this wholesome truth : 'Sin being the greatest of all evils, the sorrow for having committed it must be the greatest of all sorrows.' In this teaching we not only agree with one another, but also with holy writ, which says, 'He that covereth his sins shall not prosper, but whoso confesseth and forsaketh them shall have mercy.'"

"But," interrupted Nora, "I have always thought that Protestants did not believe at all in the confession of sins ; so, at least, I have been taught by our priests."

"Most assuredly we do ; we not only believe in it, but practise it."

"What! in the confessional, to the ears of a priest?"

"O no, not that. And here our agreement with Romanists on this subject ceases ; but let us discuss it in the light of reason and revelation."

"But I should like to know," said Luella

" what the Romish Church teaches with regard to confession."

"My Catechism and parents taught me as follows: 'That confession is a declaration which one makes of his sins to a priest, in order to obtain pardon or absolution.' Such a confession is considered a very solemn thing, and is called the 'sacrament of penance.' It is said to be necessary to salvation, except in extreme cases. It must be 'humble, sincere, and entire.' Not only is each sin to be revealed, but also the number of times each sin has been committed either in thought, word, or deed, with every attendant circumstance, including even dreams, with their effect upon waking thoughts and actions. Purposely to neglect to confess any sin, or even to forget a sin or grave circumstance of a sin for want of sufficient self-examination, would in either case constitute a sacrilege.* In order to guard this point, numerous stories like the following are related in nearly all their books of instruction to the young: 'A young lady of eighteen was guilty of a secret sin which she was ashamed to confess. She was soon brought upon a bed of death, where she was tormented and in despair. She died, and three days after she appeared to one of her friends in

* Dr. Challoner's "Catholic Instructed," p. 101.

a vision and spoke these words, 'Do not pray any more for me, sister,' (this friend supposed her to be in purgatory,) 'I am damned on account of a sin committed alone. I might have easily obtained pardon by confessing it, but a criminal shame always led me to conceal it; and thus in abusing confession and the blood of Jesus Christ, I have brought upon myself the deepest damnation.' She then uttered a groan and dispppeared.'"

"It is also currently reported among college students," said Monsieur Grenier, "that if one is inclined to hide a sin from the priest, the confessor presently sees a huge serpent's head protruding from the sinner's mouth, and in case the sin is not confessed, the serpent is withdrawn into the bosom of the wretch who dares thus attempt to deceive God. Then if he persists in communing unworthily, the wafer will be metamorphosed into an ugly toad (*un crapaud difforme*) on his tongue."

"Hence you can judge," I continued, "that to make a thorough confession must require several days of careful study, compelling one to consult the long lists of questions for self-examination to be found in nearly all the prayer-books. To assist the memory some persons carefully write a catalogue of their sins, though they are not permitted to hand this black account to the priests, for with their own lips they must declare it in his ear."

"But I should think people would get so frightened on these occasions," said Johnnie, "as to forget about all they ever did or thought."

"In order to avoid the confusion as far as possible, children are sent to the confessional very young, and often simply that they may learn how to perform or behave when they come to the thing in earnest. They are also thoroughly instructed beforehand by their parents and teachers, and the confessionals are generally so arranged as to hide them entirely from the view of others, while the priest can be seen only through a narrow grate at which he puts his ear. Then, versed as he is in all the prevailing sins of the day and place, he is well prepared to give the penitent a thorough catechising, which most priests always do. In this way treacherous memories are quickened."

"O, I remember that you showed us two confessionals in St. Joseph's," said Luella. "They looked like large portable wardrobes, with a partition through the middle, making two little rooms, with a small grate between them, about opposite to the head of a person sitting in a chair."

"You have described them perfectly. Sometimes, however, they consist of one apartment,

enclosed by a thick curtain. I have myself
frequently been to confession in such a place,
where I knelt right by the side of the priest.
'Kirwan,' in his letters to Bishop Hughes,
giving some of his early impressions upon this
subject, says, 'Father M. frequently held his
confessions at our house. He sat in a dark
room upstairs with one or more candles on a
table before him. Those going to confession
followed each other on their knees from the
front door, through the hall, up the stairs, and to
the door of the room. My turn came ; I entered
the room, from which the light of day was
excluded, and bowed myself before the priest.
He made over me the sign of the cross, and
after saying something in Latin, he ordered me
to commence the detail of my sins. 'Such was
my fright that my memory soon failed in bringing up my past delinquencies. He would prompt
me, and ask, Did you do this thing, or that
thing ? I would answer yes, or no. And when I
could say no more, he would wave his hand over
me and again utter some words in Latin, and
dismiss me.' Thus, like 'Kirwan,' I was sent
many times to confession when I was young, and
as I was quick to learn I soon became very
thorough and accurate. And though the law of
the Church requires confession but once a year,
enjoining it as a special duty of the Lenten

season, I followed the example of those who confess nearly every week."

" All this accords perfectly with my own experience," said Monsieur Grenier, " but really I would like to know what Protestants teach about confession."

" Simply this, that we are to confess to the being or person whom we have offended. This is the only rule of Scripture, and it accords perfectly with reason. ' Confess your faults one to another,' said James. This compels the priest to confess to the people, as well as the people to him. The rule is further explained by our Saviour as follows : ' If thy brother shall trespass against thee, go and tell him his fault between thee and him alone.' Not a word is to be said to the Church, including its pastor, until all other means have failed, and then the whole Church is to be a witness, or sit as a jury. In His Sermon on the Mount Christ said, 'Therefore if thou bring thy gift to the altar and there rememberest that thy brother hath aught against thee, leave there thy gift before the altar, and go thy way; first be reconciled to thy brother.' Now the priest is supposed to be at the altar, but this command sends him away from the altar to confess to his brother and be reconciled, without the interference of the priest. Again, we read in the Gospel,

'Then came Peter to Him and said, Lord, how oft shall my brother sin against me and I forgive him? till seven times?' Mark, that Peter speaks of personal offences. Jesus tells him that in such cases he must forgive 'seventy times seven.'"

"What, father," quickly inquired Johnnie, "four hundred and ninety times?"

"Yes, my son. This is probably the product of 'sacred numbers,' as they are called, meaning that in no case are we to retain resentment toward a sincere penitent. This is further illustrated in the Lord's prayer by the petition, 'Forgive us our trespasses as we forgive them that trespass against us.'"

"These passages evidently relate to offences between man and man," again said Monsieur Grenier, "in which satisfaction or restitution is to be made; but how is it with sins against a community?"

"Apply the rule given before: Confession must be made to the community. And only this kind of confession, except in case of personal offences, was known even in the Roman Catholic Church until the days of Pope Leo the Great.*

"And was he indeed the first?" spoke Monsieur Grenier, quite indignantly, "who delivered over

* See the following authorities: Bingham, *Orig. Eccl.*, book xviii., chap. iii. *Daillé, De Confess. Auricular*, iv. 25, etc.

the conscience of the people into the hands of the priests, and consigned the most secret acts and thoughts of individual imperfection to the torture of private inquisition and scrutiny ! "

"And yet," I added, " the present authorities of the Church quote the following passages in answer to the question, ' What Scripture do you bring to recommend the confession of our sins to God's ministers ?' * Here is the first : 'When a man or woman shall commit any sin that men commit, to do a trespass against the Lord, and that person be guilty, then they shall confess their sin which they have done.' Num., v., 6, 7. Now, as no priest is mentioned in this passage, unless auricular confession can be proved from some other passage it does not answer the above question, but serves only to mislead. But auricular confession cannot be maintained from the Old Testament ; hence the Rev. Dr. Challoner has misapplied the word of God, as the above confession was undoubtedly public. The second passage he adduces is the example of the people who came to John the Baptist, and were baptized of him, ' confessing their sins.' Matt., iii., 6. Now, we may ask, if this was auricular confession, of whom had John learned the practice, and where was his confessional, with

* Challoner's "Catholic Instructed," pp. 99, 100.

time to attend to these multitudes ? St. Luke, in the third chapter of his Gospel, makes the whole matter simple, by representing the people generally, then the publicans, and lastly the soldiers, as asking, 'And what shall we do ? ' Their confessions were evidently public, as their offences had been, and as were also his instructions to them.   Dr. Challoner brings forward also that injunction of James, 'Confess your faults one to another '—a passage which I have already sufficiently explained—and concludes his answer with this text : 'And many that believed came, and confessed, and showed their deeds.' Acts, xix., 18. This case at Ephesus was very similar to that of John the Baptist at Jordan, and is susceptible of a like explanation. There is not the least intimation of confession to a priest or an apostle, nor of confession in private, but rather of a public and open acknowledgment."

"But what of offences against God only ? " inquired Nora, who had been listening with intense interest.

"Apply the rule already given, Nora, for it is invariable and simple. If you offend God only, confess to God only. The Psalmist David confessed, crying, 'Against thee, thee only, have I sinned, and done this evil in thy sight.' In another passage he exclaims, 'I acknowleged my sin unto thee, and my iniquity have I not hid. I said, I will confess my transgressions unto the Lord, and thou forgavest the iniquity of my sin.' "

"I see that no priest appears here between God and man; but this was the rule of Old Testament times," said Nora.

" Christ the crucified is the Alpha and Omega of the new dispensation. In the olden time the priests occupied a much more imposing relation than the ministers of Christ do now, though never that of confessors. They received and offered the sacrifices of the people, and made prayers and supplications for them. But all those ceremonies, as also the priest and the sacrifice, were only types of Christ, pointing to him, and they were fulfilled, abolished, and lost in him. And so the Apostle Paul, in all his epistles, and especially in that to the Hebrews, many of whom clung so tenaciously to the old ritual, most conclusively proves that Christ is not only exalted far above angels, Abraham, Moses, and even Aaron and his lineal priesthood, but that by his vicarious sufferings and sacrificial death he has forever abolished the 'law of carnal ordinances,' that is, the law of a human priesthood and of animal offerings; and that now, having offered one sacrifice for sins forever, that is, one never to be repeated, himself the Victim and Offerer, he has become our only priest, the true shepherd and bishop of our souls, able to save them to the uttermost that come unto God by Him, seeing He ever liveth to make intercession for them; made a high-priest forever after the order of Melchisedek, not after the law of a carnal commandment, but after the power of an endless life."

"How delighted I am," (*que je suis charmé*,) exclaimed Monsieur Grenier, "to be told what it now seems to me must be the substance of those sacred writings of Paul which, though twenty-three years of age, I have never read! These truths not only show that priestly intervention between a soul and God is positively unscriptural, but also that the so-called sacrifice of the mass, which the Catechism teaches is 'the offering of the body and blood of Jesus Christ, made by a priest unto God,' or 'that in the mass there is offered to God a true, and proper propitiatory sacrifice for the living and the dead,' *— that such a service, of which the Roman Catholic Church makes so much, is unmeaning, if not farcical, and calculated to hide the great and all-sufficient sacrifice of Calvary behind the rubbish of priestly power and ritualistic gibberish."

"Be this as it may," I added, "the mass, with its priestly sacrifices, is plainly anti-scriptural. Our Saviour himself, and his apostles after him,

* "Grounds of Catholic Faith," p. 43.

endeavoured to show this by removing every object or person that might possibly obscure or obstruct spiritual communion between God and man. In his parable of the Prodigal Son the Saviour represents the penitent one as coming directly to the Father. Prostrate 1 fore him he confesses, 'Father, I have sinned a᷉ ...ist heaven and before thee.' Where is the priest to hear his confession? He is not even so much as named, in this pearl of parables, this gospel in the Gospel, nor anywhere else in the Scriptures, in the relation of confessor between the sinner and his God. Paul sets the royal seal to this subject when he says, 'There is one God, and *one* Mediator between God and man, the man Christ Jesus.' And Peter adds, 'Neither is there salvation in any other; for there is none other name under heaven given among men, whereby we must be saved.' "

With these good texts to meditate upon, after a brief season of prayer, our interview was closed.

VII.

POWER OF THE CONFESSIONAL—NORA IN TROUBLE—
TERRIBLE ESPIONAGE — ARROGANCE OF POWER—
"WHATSOEVER YE SHALL BIND ON EARTH, ETC."—
THIS THE GORDIAN KNOT—DIOGENES — BLESSED
LAMB OF CALVARY.

All power is given unto me in heaven and in earth.—Our High Priest.

IN the early part of the week Nora had received a letter from her parents, who reside in New York city, calling her home in haste to see her mother, who was reported to be dangerously ill. She returned Friday, and, what was not a little strange, instead of going to work as usual, she came directly to my room, where she found me engaged in study. She appeared pleased at first to see me, passed the compliments of the day, but with a strange air remarked that her mother was not sick as they had written her, but that this was done as a ruse to get her home. I quickly saw that something was wrong; so desiring to talk over the matter, I asked her to sit down a moment, which she did, but in doing so she buried her face in her hands and began to weep.

"What is the matter, Nora?" I asked; "is there anything that I can do for you?"

"O no, sir," she replied, almost choking with her sobs, "but I have come in to tell you that I can work for you no longer, but must leave you;" and she sobbed again, and aloud.

After waiting some minutes for her great grief to subside, I asked, "Nora, is the work too hard for you here, or is your pay insufficient?"

"O no, sir. With all these I am perfectly satisfied."

"Has any member of the family—myself, the mistress, or the children—in any way abused or offended you?"

"No, indeed! I was never treated with more uniform kindness in my life."

"Why is it, then, that you want to leave us?"

"O, sir, I have not said that *I wanted* to leave you, but that I *must*." So saying, she again began to weep violently.

"Now, Nora, I confess I can scarcely understand you. There appears to be a mystery hanging over this matter. I cannot think, however, that you are willing to leave us without even intimating it beforehand, as was the understanding you should do when you came here, and without assigning any reasons why."

8

"O, how can I ever tell you, though I know I ought to!" And here, seemingly absorbed with her own griefs, and as though she were alone, she exclaimed, "O, holy St. Patrick, patron and protector of my people, why am I left to be the prey of torments like these!"

"Never mind St. Patrick now, nor any other saint, Nora. Try to get quiet; put your trust in the blessed Jesus, and do what you know is right, and you will find that rest to your conscience which you cannot otherwise obtain. If you feel that for the sake of truth, for our sake, and your own, you ought to tell us all about this trouble, do so plainly."

By this time Mrs. Beaudry, who from the hall had heard Nora's sobs, had come in, and, learning that her grief was caused by feeling herself, as it were, forced to leave us, became greatly interested in the matter.

The troubled girl hesitated for some time, but at length a radiance seemed to light upon her face, though swollen with tears and grief, as when a summer shower is speedily followed by golden sunbeams that light up the last fallen raindrops into gems of beauty, and gild the trail of the retiring clouds; and then, like one who has reached a great victory in a moral struggle, she exclaimed, "I somehow begin to feel as though I had suffered my conscience to be trampled under foot by others, while it seems as if God alone ought to be above conscience. I certainly can't tell you exactly why, but now I feel quite free to tell you all about this thing which has caused me so much grief, and awakened, I see, great anxiety in your own minds."

"That's right, Nora," said Mrs. Beaudry; "speak the truth, the whole truth, and nothing but the truth."

"I'll try, ma'am. A few days before I received the letter telling me the story of mother's sickness, some Roman Catholic friends—no, I'll call them enemies—in the neighbourhood, who had found out that I was becoming interested in those talks of Mr. Beaudry on his experience, wrote to my parents, telling them all about it. When I reached home I found my mother in tears—she was really sick at heart—and my father was so angry that he made all manner of threats against me, if I wouldn't go and confess it all to our parish priest. I hesitated some time, but at length went. O what a horrid experience I had there! Of course, according to the rules of our Church, I didn't dare hide anything from him."

"Nor need you violate any obligation of secrecy in the confessional for our sakes, Nora," I added, lest her conscience might become unnecessarily entangled.

"But I must tell you the whole story to relieve my own mind, and lest you blame me for saying that I must leave you. One of the first things the priest did was to inquire all about you. He then said he had heard of you before, and of many others the likes of you throughout the country. After asking me many questions concerning your religion, and your meetings in the study, all about which he seemed to know beforehand, I tried to tell him that, by what I had seen in your family, I thought you must be a good Christian man, when he grew into a hot rage, and, interrupting me, cried, 'Hush, you almost-Protestant! You utter blasphemy! Talk about a good heretic! You might as well say a *pious devil.* That man is a turncoat, a Judas,' and thus he went on talking, and he looked so angrily at me that I fairly trembled; and he ordered me to leave your family at once, or he would call all the curses of God to fall upon me. I was so frightened, that to obtain his absolution I promised to do as he commanded me. Now this is the cause of my tears, for I had rather do anything I know of than to leave you:" and again a cloud of sorrow seemed to fall upon her.

"But, Nora," I proceeded to say, "do as you think is right. Obey God rather than man. If

conscience says ' Go,' don't waver, though it will
be a great sacrifice for us all."

"You are very kind to speak so to me; but,
O, that I only knew what to do?" After some
moments of silent thoughtfulness she joyfully
exclaimed, "I know what to do. I'll not go
and leave you. I just now recollect seeing
in some of our Catechisms, that if a person
through fear or compulsion should make a
rash vow, it is only adding sin to sin to keep
such a promise. I'll do right, at any cost of
pain or loss, God helping me."

At this interesting *dénouement* she made each
of us a polite courtesy, and smiling, retired to
her room.

"Now, Pearlie," (for this is Mrs. Beaudry's
given name), "what do you think of priestly
power?"

"Why, I had no conception of it before. Now
I see by what means the priests obtain their
wide information and great influence. Their
operations of espionage, I can now imagine, are
reduced to a system so perfect that there is not
a person of wealth, or social standing, or
political or religious influence in the land, who
may not be perfectly well known at head-
quarters, even to the minutest thing in his history or conduct. The confessional is the channel
of this information."

So saying, she went out to attend to her domestic cares, leaving me alone to meditate upon this strange yet not uncommon event. Nora continued to work as usual, only with an increasing interest.

These facts being known to our company greatly enlisted our sympathy for Nora, and enlivened our interest in the general subject of discussion. On assembling the following Sabbath, Aunt Melie remarked, "There is still another subject connected with the confessional on which I would like more light: and that is, the power of the priest to forgive sins. Most Roman Catholics with whom I have conversed have told me that the priest has this power, and that it is absolute; others surround the doctrine with various limitations; while still others deny it altogether."

"Their standard books," I replied, "are our only safe authority in these matters." Turning to Monsieur Grenier, who was again with us, I asked him if he could repeat from memory what his Catechism taught upon this subject.

"Most certainly. It is only a short time since I was devoutly studying and teaching these doctrines. In the Catechism now in use in Canada, I think on page 51, you may find the following questions and answers :—

"'Have the priests power to forgive sins?'

" 'Yes, the priests have power to forgive or retain sins.'

" 'Can they forgive all sins, even the most enormous ?'

" 'Yes, they can pardon all sins, even the most enormous, provided they are confessed with sincere contrition.' "

"Well," exclaimed Luella, "this is claiming even more power than Jesus himself did, for he said there was one sin he could not forgive, namely, the sin against the Holy Ghost; but the priests makes no such exception."

"This is most poignantly true," continued our friend. "But the Catechism does not contain their whole teaching on this point. In a book* used in college I found the following: 'To remit sins, to bind and to loose consciences, to produce the body and blood of Jesus Christ, to offer him in sacrifice, to distribute him to the faithful, to impart grace by the sacraments to the living and the dying, to cast out devils: this is what all the kings of the earth cannot do ; but behold, this is what the priests of the Lord can do.' Then, too, in the voluminous works of Abbé Jean Gaume, works approved by Romish authority, and highly recommended, I have found the following: 'What human tongue can describe

* "Pensées sur les Vérités de la Religion," p. 297.

the dignity of the priesthood and the greatness
of the priests?' Then the author proceeds to
speak of the power of Adam, Moses, Joshua, of
kings, of angels, and even of the Virgin Mary,
but says, 'The priest has greater power than
them all, because they cannot, while he can,
absolve a soul from sin.' He continues: 'Suppose
the Redeemer should visibly descend in person
in his Church, and station himself in a confessional to administer the sacrament of penance,
while a priest occupies another. The Son of God
says, "I absolve you;" and the priest also says,
"I absolve you;" and the penitent finds himself
absolved just as much by the one as by the
other. Thus the priest, mighty like God, can
instantly snatch the sinner from hell, render
him worthy of paradise, and of a slave of the
devil make him a child of Abraham, and God
himself is obliged to submit to the judgment of
the priest, to refuse or to grant absolution,
provided the penitent is worthy of it. The
sentence of the priest precedes; God subscribes
to it. Can any one conceive of a greater power,
a higher dignity?'

"And yet these sentiments of the Abbé are
not as radical as the utterances of a Bavarian
priest, named Herr Kinzelmann, Roman Catholic
rector of Gestrass. In a recent sermon preached
at Algau, and reported in the *Kempton Gazette,*

he said: 'We priests, we are above the governments, above the emperors, kings, and princes, as much as the heavens are above the earth. The kings and princes of the earth are as far behind us priests as lead is distant from the purest gold. The angels and archangels are much below priests; for we can, in the face of God, pardon sins, which they have never been able to do. We are above the Mother of God, for Mary never gave birth to Christ but once, while we priests, we create and produce him every day. Again, to a certain degree, the priests are above God himself; for God must be, at any time and in every place, at our disposal; he must, on being ordered, descend from heaven at the consecration of the mass. God, it is true, has created the world by using these words: 'Be it;' but we, with these words, create God himself.' "

"Thank you, Monsieur Grenier, for the information I desired," replied Aunt Melie. "But is it not dreadful to contemplate such arrogance of power! It is the legitimate fruit of the system, however. Here we see the fulfilment of Paul's prophecy concerning 'the falling away, and the revelation of that man of sin and son of perdition, who opposeth and exalteth himself above all that is called God, or that is worshipped; so that he as God sitteth in the temple of God, showing himself that he is God.'"

"Now," added Nora, "I have always been made to believe that the priests have all power. If the priests cannot pardon sin, I should like to know who can?"

As she uttered these words, as a matter of course, all eyes were turned toward me for an answer, and so I replied, "All Scriptures bearing upon this question teach us that the pardoning power resides with God alone. So David said, 'Thou forgavest the iniquity of my sin.' John, 'If we confess our sins, He is faithful and just to forgive us our sins.' The same is true in a civil point of view. Before the law an offender can be pardoned only by the chief magistrate having jurisdiction, the Governor in the State, the President in the United States. So Jesus Christ, who is Lord of lords and King of kings, alone has the power to forgive him who has trespassed upon his divine law. So when Christ had said to the paralytic, 'Thy sins be forgiven thee,' the Pharisees murmured against him, and exclaimed, 'Who can forgive sins but God only?' This passage proves two things: first, that priestly absolutions formed no part of the Jewish creed; and, secondly, that if Christ had been only a man, the Pharisees would have been justified in charging blasphemy upon him. But then, to show forth his supreme d'vinity in the presence of them all, Jesus said, 'Whether is it easier to

say to the sick of the palsy, Thy sins be forgiven thee; or to say, Arise, and take up thy bed
and walk ? But that ye may know that the Son
of man hath power on earth to forgive sins, (he
saith to the sick of the palsy,) I say unto thee,
Arise, and take up thy bed, and go thy way
unto thy house.' And it was immediately done.
Both by his reasoning and action Jesus proved
in this instance, as in many others, that to forgive sins and to work miracles, such as healing
the sick, raising the dead, etc., are on a par with
creating worlds, and that these are prerogatives
of the Deity which he has never delegated to
men. He may work a miracle by man as an
instrument, as he says, 'he can thrash a mountain with a worm;' but the power does not
belong to the instrument, but to the arm that
wields it."

"But your words remind me of two passages
of Scripture often quoted by the priests," interrupted Monsieur Grenier, "which present questions that to my mind are not yet clearly
answered."

"Please state them," I said.

"They are the words of Christ to his apostles,
as recorded, I think, in the gospels by Matthew
and John. The first is, 'Whatsoever ye shall
bind on earth shall be bound in heaven; and
whatsoever ye shall loose on earth shall be

loosed in heaven.' The second is much like the first, namely, 'Receive ye the Holy Ghost whosoever sins ye remit, they are remitted unto them; and whosoever sins ye retain, they are retained.' The priests tell us that Christ here delegated all the power that he had in heaven and earth to them."

"Father!" said Johnnie, his countenance showing no small amount of perplexity, " I fear you've got a puzzle this time which you cannot very easily unravel."

"Dispel your fears on my behalf, my child. You must learn that many things which appear difficult, and even impossible, to you now, will become perfectly simple after long study and experience. These passages plainly mean this: That the Gospel truth committed to the apostles, accompanied by the Holy Ghost whom Jesus then breathed upon them, and whom they fully received at the pentecost, is the power by which men are to be saved. Look at the unequivocal testimony of Jesus and his apostles on the subject: 'Then said Jesus to those Jews which believed on him, If ye continue in my word, then ye are my disciples indeed; and ye shall know the truth, and the truth shall make you free.' Again, in his prayer for the apostles just before his crucifixion, he said, ' Father, sanctify them through thy truth ; thy word is truth.' In his final commission to them he said, 'Go ye into all the world and preach the Gospel to every creature. He that believeth and is baptized shall be saved; but he that believeth not shall be damned.' "

"O! I see it, I see it now," almost shouted Monsieur Grenier, quite in a rhapsody; "whether a man be saved or lost depends upon his either receiving by faith, or rejecting the Gospel."

"That's it exactly. It is a simple truth, but mighty."

"Why! you said before, it is God forgives sins; now you say men are saved through the truth," said Nora, somewhat perplexed.

"The truth, by whomsoever it is made known, Nora, is the voice of God. Hear what Paul says about it: 'The Gospel is the power of God unto salvation to every one that believeth.' Again, 'So we preach, and so ye believe.' Peter offers his testimony as follows, and certainly you ought to consider that valid: 'Seeing ye have purified your souls in obeying the truth through the Spirit....Being born again, not of corruptible seed, but incorruptible; by the word of God, which liveth and abideth forever.' Jesus further taught, 'If I had not come and spoken unto them, they had not had sin, but now they have no cloak for their sin.' So you see that no small responsibility is thrown upon the hearer of the Gospel. If we believe and obey the truth, our sins are forgiven, and we are cleansed from all unrighteousness, by the power of God speaking to us in the truth; but if we reject the truth, our sins are not only retained against us in heaven, but our guilt is greatly increased by our knowledge. 'To the one,' then says Paul, 'we are a savour of death unto death, and to the other a savour of life unto life.' No minister of the Gospel is more than a feeble instrument in the hands of God in accomplishing this work. If I bring water to a man who is almost dying of thirst—he may say that I saved his life, but it was God's pure beverage that did it. The priest is not the water nor the bread of life; he can only tell of them or distribute them. The knowledge of this grace is the key which Christ is said to have given to Peter, and which, though abused, he tells us was nevertheless in the hands of the Jewish people. He said to them, 'Woe unto you, lawyers! for ye have taken away the key of knowledge: ye entered not in yourselves, and them that were entering in ye hindered.' The parallel passage in Matthew amplifies the thought: 'Woe unto you, Scribes and Pharisees, hypocrites! for ye shut the kingdom of heaven against men: for ye neither go in yourselves, neither suffer ye them

that **are** entering to go in.' These woes were
pronounced upon them because they not only
rejected Christ and his Gospel, but sought to
prevent others from receiving him. But the
passages show that Gospel truth is the key of
the kingdom of God. Whosoever receives the
truth in the love of it enters in. The key, then,
is not only in the hands of Peter, or with the
ministers of the Gospel, but in the hands of all
men who know the truth."

"But did not Christ design to convey more
power to the Twelve than to other believers ? "
asked Monsieur Grenier.

"Only in this: They were to. decide, in
council assembled, as we see in the Acts of the
Apostles, what doctrines were orthodox, and
they were made the custodians or superinten-
dents of discipline in the Church. Paul explains
the relation of the Apostles to the churches as
follows : ' Not for that *we have dominion over
your faith*, but are helpers of your joy: for by
faith ye stand.' And Peter adds, in his epistle,
speaking to the elders : ' Feed the flock of God
which is among you, taking the oversight
thereof, not by constraint, but willingly ; not for
filthy lucre, but of a ready mind ; *neither
as being lords over God's heritage*, but being
ensamples to the flock.' And it is further
evident that all their decisions were in accor-

dance with a vote of the whole Church or flock. But the only keys that open heaven and hell are in the hands of Jesus, who is heard saying to the revelator, 'I am he that liveth, and was dead; and behold, I am alive for evermore, amen; and have the keys of hell and of death.'"

"I question somewhat, after hearing your remarks," said Mrs. Beaudry, "whether the title of priest belongs to a Christian minister."

"I am sure it does not," I replied. "The prophet of the Old Testament was a type of the preacher of the New; the priest was a type of Christ. The great Master said to his apostles, 'Go and preach the Gospel, teaching those who believe to observe all things whatsoever I have commanded you.' So Paul says, 'Christ sent me not to baptize, but to preach the Gospel,' 'for we preach not ourselves, but Christ Jesus the Lord; and ourselves your servants,' (not your priests and lords,) 'for Jesus' sake,' and 'we have this treasure in earthen vessels that the excellency of the power may be of God, and not of us.' The minister is not the way—he may simply indicate it by word and deed. He cannot pardon sin, but he can point out the Pardoner. He is simply the voice of one, and that voice an echo from heaven, crying in the wilderness of the world, 'Behold the Lamb of God!' Like a crystal drop in the sky, hidden from mortal gaze, yet so controlled by the divine Artist as to paint the resplendent rainbow, that golden girdle of the Almighty, upon the brow of evening; so the minister of Christ is to be merely a reflector of God's truth and glory. A tongue of fire to speak of God was not only the stupendous miracle of the pentecost, but it is the fittest symbol for the Gospel ministry, the talisman of the new covenant. Only Christ can say, 'Unto me all power is given,' therefore 'come unto me all ye that labour and are heavy laden;' for him hath God exalted with his right hand to be a Prince and a Saviour, for to give repentance to Israel and forgiveness of sins.'"

"Now, then," added Luella, "is fulfilled the word of Christ: 'As Moses lifted up the serpent in the wilderness, even so must the Son of man be lifted up, that whosoever believeth in him shall not perish, but have eternal life.'"

"And, indeed, is this all there is of salvation," cried Monsieur Grenier, "to look to the Crucified and Risen One, and live?"

"That is all," I replied. "There is life for a look at the Crucified One, for he says, 'Look unto me, and be ye saved, all the ends of the earth: for I am God, and there is none else,' The minister's duty, then, is simply to cry, 'Behold the Lamb,' and to stand aside or hide away, lest he should attract or obstruct the

9

sinner's gaze. There was beauty and force in the remark of the philosopher Diogenes to Alexander the Great, who stood in his sunshine when he was asked by the latter what he wanted. The cynic replied, 'I want you to stand out of my sunshine, and not to take from me what you cannot give me.' The sinner must be left alone with his God." Inspired by these simple yet weighty truths, we closed our interview with this appropriate stanza, each one singing with strange delight:—

> ' I am trusting, Lord, in thee;
> Blessed Lamb of Calvary !
> Humbly at thy cross I bow—
> Jesus saves me, saves me now."

VIII.

THE CONFESSIONAL ON PRIEST AND PEOPLE—WHO CAN
JUDGE THE CONSCIENCE?—POLITICAL ARGUMENT—
MORAL INFLUENCE—COUNCIL OF TRENT—PEOPLE IN
ABJECT FEAR—SECRETS—WEAKNESS.

*Be not deceived: evil communications corrupt good manners.—Paul
to the Corinthians.*

THE time had been so short since our last
assembly, that meeting the same persons
in the same place, and under similar
circumstances, made it seem as if this
gathering was only a continuation of
the previous one. Our preliminaries were very
brief, for every one appeared so anxious to enter
the confessional, not to confess their sins, but to
draw from me the information which I had
partly pledged myself to give, that I was compelled to begin at once, which I did as follows:

"Auricular confession, as introduced by Pope
Leo, was so evidently a corruption of apostolical teaching and practice, that it took many
years to enforce it throughout the Church. The

Irish Church particularly long withstood the innovation. But now the authorities of the Church endeavour—how successfully has already been shown—to prove the practice from Scripture; but conscious of the weakness of their position, they resort to what they call 'The spiritual benefits of the sacrament of penance.'"

"Pray tell us what these benefits are," said Luella.

Before I had time to answer, the door-bell was rung. Nora ran down, and soon returned with a card, which bore the well-known autograph of "Mr. W." He was a descendant of Pennsylvania Quakers, a graduate of Yale College, and had spent the two years following his graduation in the study of law. But when he came to enter upon the practice of it he found so much trickery in the profession that his conscientious scruples did not allow him to continue therein. After spending some time in foreign travel he devoted himself to teaching, in which avocation he had few superiors. He was now the principal of our school, and familiarly named "Professor."

I went down to the parlour and met him. As I entered, he arose and said, "Though not a member of any Church, I do not believe in Sunday calls, agreeing perfectly with your sentiments on that subject as expressed in your morning discourse. But from a few remarks I heard from Miss Luella and her brother at school, I feel a deep interest in the Sunday afternoon interviews now held in your family, and I have come to request the privilege of being a listener, if it be not asking too much, or intruding upon sacred privacies."

"You are welcome, Professor, not only as an auditor, but as a full participant in our conversations. Thus far, at least, there has been nothing said which we are not willing should be widely known. Come up, please, to the study with me, and I trust you may be able to impart as well as to receive instruction."

The Professor scarcely needed an introduction, except to Monsieur Grenier, and, because of his affable yet unobtrusive manners, every one felt perfectly at home in his presence. Taking a seat, he asked pardon for having interrupted us, and expressed the hope that he might not again be guilty of a like offence.

I told him that we had just commenced our conversation, and that the bell rang just as I was about to answer Luella's question as to what were the so-called benefits of the sacrament of penance, or the moral influence of auricular confession. He nodded assent, as much as to say, this question perfectly suits me, and I began: "There is, no doubt, a certain class in the Church upon which this practice has, at least for a time, a salutary influence. They are restrained from the grosser vices by the dread they have of the upbraidings of their confessor, accompanied, it may be, with his refusal of absolution. A youth of my acquaintance, who was enticed to the commission of a great sin, replied, 'Wait till after Easter, when I have made my confession and communed.' Many also fear the penances which are always enjoined, even though absolution is granted. These consist in frequent repetition of lengthy prayers, or in reading the 'seven penitential psalms,' which Galileo was compelled to recite every week for three years in succession, or in protracted and painful fastings. Sometimes public humiliations are imposed, such as was inflicted upon a school-mate of mine, who was compelled to kneel in the middle of the broad central aisle of the church, where everybody could see him, and where he remained during the entire service of the mass, for at least an hour, with his head bowed almost to the floor. This was repeated several times. Occasionally the penance consists in going barefoot on long pilgrimages, or with peas or something else in one's shoes to hurt or annoy. Frequently such sufferings are self-imposed; and some have gone so far as to severely flog themselves, or even to wear a wide iron girdle tight around their body, producing excruciating torture."

"I had an uncle," said Nora, "who nearly killed himself by doing penance. He was a very devoted man, and we sometimes called him a saint."

" Furthermore," I continued, " the confessional has sometimes assisted in recovering stolen property. For instance, a lady of my acquaintance, by the name of Forsyth, residing in Keeseville, N. Y., had a brass kettle stolen by her washer-woman, as she supposed, who, however, denied the charge. Mrs. F. reported her conviction to the parish priest, whom she knew. The first time this wayward penitent appeared in the confessional, the priest, of course, watched for the brass kettle. The woman seemed to have closed her confession, when the priest asked, 'And is there nothing more?' 'Nothing more, my ghostly father,' she replied. 'Hark!' said the priest, 'what sound is this I hear like the rattling of a brass kettle?' Nothing more was necessary. Overwhelmed by her superstitious dread of the priest's supposed supernatural knowledge and power, she confessed the whole, and the next morning Mrs. Forsyth found her kettle by the kitchen door."

" Don't you wish we could be as successful in

finding the linen which was taken by our washer-woman?" asked Luella.

"Certainly; but the remedy is not always so sure as in this instance."

"But is there no spiritual good in the confessional?" inquired Mrs. Beaudry.

"Undoubtedly; there are times when persons under peculiar temptations or weaknesses may be properly advised or assisted."

"But are these advantages sufficient to compensate for what we know to be its evils?" asked Aunt Melie.

"By no means. Now, in order the better to understand the subject, let us look, first, at the influence of the confessional on the priest. The supernatural power with which it is assumed he is invested is enough to fill any human heart with pride, and to intoxicate any brain with self-conceit. Arrayed in the insignia of his authority, he sits in the confessional as a god upon a throne of judgment, and not as a man. In the book called 'Grounds,' page 29—and there is no better papal authority—it is written: 'Christ has made the pastors of his Church his judges in the court of conscience, with commission and authority to bind or loose, to forgive or to retain sins, according to the merits of the cause, and the disposition of the penitents. Now, as no judge can pass sentence without a full knowledge of the cause—which cannot be had in this kind of causes which regard men's consciences but by their own confession—it clearly follows, that he who has made the pastors of his Church the judges of men's consciences, has also laid an obligation upon the faithful to lay open the state of their consciences to them, if they hope to have their sins remitted.' "

" Now, I see," said the Professor, " as I never saw before, the secret spring of power in the Romish Church ! It explains to me many a phenomenon which I had witnessed, and for which I could find no adequate cause. This teaching places the confessional above all civil and above all religious powers, and the priest above every earthly ruler. For by his word, spoken in the tribunal of conscience, he can abrogate the fealty of subjects to their king, cancel a civil obligation, or annul a judicial oath. He can even sever the marriage ties ! Indeed, there is no mischief that he cannot do, if he be so disposed. When I consider that millions of dollars' worth of church property and real estate are in their hands, and vast sums of floating capital which they control, besides their annual incomes, which must be immense, I can see how it is, that adding their monetary to their ministerial power, they wield so tremendous an influence in the realm of politics. As they seldom make speeches or publish letters on the subject in this country—the same thing cannot be said of them in Canada, however, nor in Mexico, nor even in Ireland, nor France, where I witnessed their operations—I could not conjecture how they reached the masses; but the confessional reveals the hiding of their power. But I am consuming too much of your precious time with these remarks."

"Not at all, Professor. They are directly to the point, and no man is better fitted to make them than yourself. Continue, if you please."

"I have but this to say now, that I cannot see how a priest, or even a private member of the Church, can honestly take the oath of naturalization in this country, when it is admitted that the consciences of the masses are in the hands of the priests (which they themselves acknowledge), and that the priests themselves are controlled under solemn vows and religious oaths, by a close ecclesiastical corporation having the Roman Pontiff at its head. Every foreigner who desires to be naturalized is required to declare on oath, in open court, 'that it is *bona fide* his intention to become a citizen of the United States, and to renounce forever all allegiance and fidelity to any foreign prince, potentate, State, or sovereignty whatever.' Under these circumstances, I am convinced that such an oath by a Romanist is perjury, or, at least, a nullity. For there is not a Romanist, lay or clerical, but would side with the Pope of Rome in the event of a conflict with our authorities. The demoralizing influence of such oaths has been seen in the recent revelation of unparalleled frauds committed by the officials of New York city nearly all of whom were Romanists, and all evidently under priestly control—a control exhibited in the vast sums of money and land grants which have been annually made by the city corporation to build up and extend Roman Catholic institutions within its bounds. This is true of other places also. As a lover of my country, I am jealous of these corrupting influences, exerted mostly by foreign-born citizens and priests—for nearly all their priests are imported—in the interest of a religious organization which, in form and spirit, is inimical to the genius of our institutions and government. Let foreigners worship as they think best, so long as they do not encroach upon my privileges and rights as a citizen. But let them not baptize political trickery and usurpation with the sacred name of religion. Now, I have spoken not as a religionist or a political partisan—for I am neither—but as a man."

" With your permission," I remarked, " we will consider this to be the political influence of the confessional, a topic which, without your presence, must have been wanting in our discussion. Now you can see the moral effect of such assumed power on the priest himself. His spirit being thus inflated with false conceptions of himself and of his work, think of the influence upon his heart and mind of the revelations of human depravity which he is there to solicit and receive. When he takes his position in the confessional, the 'soiled doves' of his Church come one after another in rapid succession, flocking at his feet. Claiming to have power to pardon all sins, he must first hear the recital of them. The whole heart must be opened to him. Now, the foulest thoughts ever conceived or even conceivable; the most complicated plans ever laid for robbery, seduction, and even murder; the blackest deeds that midnight ever witnessed; all the sins and crimes of childhood, manhood, womanhood, old age; on the part of the single and the married; in secret, in public, in the family, in the State, with all the attending circumstances, descending even to disgusting details, which modesty declines to tell*—all this tide of corruption is poured into the confessor's ears. To withstand such contaminating influences, one must be more than human—must

* Dens' "Theology in Latin," vol. vii., pp. 149-153, etc.

possess an impeccablé nature, which no priest even professes to have.   Peter Dens in his volume vi., p. 175, says, 'That confessor who is every day occupied in the ministry of hearing confessions, falls very seldom, in comparison with the times he does not fall.'   He speaks, of course, from personal experience.   He then proceeds in his works, which are extensively used in all clerical colleges, to present what legislation he deems necessary to redress or prevent seductions and other crimes by the priests in the confessional, acknowledging thereby that these abominations have existed and continue to exist.

"It is doubtless true, that the young and conscientious priest may at first shrink from the viper, and endeavour for a time to shield himself from the venom of its impurity; but he soon finds his hold upon his vows of chastity giving way, and ere long realizes what thousands of this class have been compelled in truth to confess, that,—

'When once a shaking monarchy declines,
   Each thing grows bold and to its fall combines.'

An inspired apostle has laid down as a cardinal truth in relation to human influence, a truth corroborated by all history, that 'evil communications corrupt good manners,' for even 'a little leaven leaveneth the whole lump.' And a poet says:

> ' Vice is a monster of so frightful mien,
>   As to be hated, needs but to be seen ;
>   Yet seen too oft, familiar with her face,
>   We first endure, *then pity*, THEN EMBRACE.'"

" But does not the Church impose restraining checks, and has she not the power," inquired the Professor, "to annul the orders and consequent authority of fallen or wicked priests ? "

"Here is what she says on this subject. In the fourteenth session of the Council of Trent, held November 25, 1551, under Pope Julius III., it was enacted as follows, and the clause has never been repealed: 'The Council further teaches, that even those priests who are living in mortal sin exercise the function of forgiving sins, as the ministers of Christ, by the power of the Holy Ghost conferred upon them in ordination; but that those who contend that wicked priests have not this power, hold very erroneous sentiments.' "

"How humiliating," exclaimed Aunt Melie, "is this confession of priestly corruption! How bold this assumption of spiritual power !"

"I have often wondered," added Nora, "how the priests get along with hearing so much wickedness. I have feared that many of them even love to hear it. I have sometimes shuddered, too, to think thát, while they teach that no one should partake of the holy communion without having just before confessed all his sins and received absolution, under pain of profanation and sacrilege, they themselves commune every time they celebrate mass, which many of them do every day, without having confessed their sins, perhaps, for a long time, and just after hearing such awful confessions as I know they must hear!"

"I propose we leave the poor priests, Nora," interrupted Luella, " and hear about the influence of the confessional on the people."

" Very well," I replied; "I think it may easily be inferred from what has already been said, that the influence of the confessional on the people is, to inspire a spirit of abject and servile submission to the priest. They know that he is in possession of every secret of their families, of their lives and hearts, themselves having been the informers. They believe, too, that he can open or shut heaven's door for or against them. Many even believe that his curse is able to metamorphose their bodies into animal forms, or to bewitch them. Hence their willingness to perform any penance he may impose, and to yield to any request he may make. All these privacies are, of course, kept under the secret seal of confession, an obligation on priest and

penitent, than which none can be more binding
and solemn.   This secret extends even to crimes
which one may intend to commit.*   I speak
from experience and observation when I say
also, that the confessional breeds a fearful license
to immorality.   A boy, whom I was reproving
for a certain sin, remarked—for we were boys
together—'O, it does not matter how often I do
this; I'll confess it to the priest and he'll make
it all right, because he can forgive many sins as
easily as a few.'   'As confession and penance are
much easier than the extirpation of sin from the
heart, and abandonment of vice in the life,' says
Dr. Merle D'Aubigné,' many cease contending
against the lusts of the flesh, and prefer gratifying them at the expense of a few mortifications.'
This spirit more or less pervades all classes, and
in many instances gives the passions unbridled
liberty."

"I had occasion to witness this very thing,"
added the Professor, " especially in Cuba and in
the South American States, where drunkenness,
licentiousness, and Sabbath desecration sweep,
in their tide of corruption, over both priests and
people."

"The confessional," I continued, "often leads
the young into the sinful practices which it

* Dens, voL vi., p. 218. Challoner's "Catholic Instructed,"
p. 102.

professes to check or to remove, and even encourage them therein. For instance, at one time, when I was in the confessional, the priest questioned me in relation to a certain class of sins which I then knew nothing about. This awakened no small excitement and curiosity in me. It led me to study, and to inquire of older boys and bolder sinners than myself, until I learned forms of wickedness which, had it not been for the confessional, I might never have known; certainly not so early."

"My testimony corroborates yours," said Monsieur Grenier, pensively, " and your remarks recall sad experiences which fill my heart with burning memories, and with bitterness against the confessional. I know it to be an enginery of political and spiritual corruption, the details of which it would be a disgrace to reveal. Here is a power which rules the conscience and stifles its voice; which creeps secretly into houses or families, and leads captive silly women and children, 'laden with sins, led away with divers lusts.' This truth I also found in the Bible."

"While my experience and sentiments agree with yours in the main," added Nora, "I was such a little mischief when very young that I was never taught anything new in the confessional; and yet the priest often asked me questions which made me blush with shame."

10

"And yet the confessional," I went on to say, "is the only door to the various privileges of the Church. The proselyte must enter the confessional before he does the Church, generally before he can be baptized. Confession stands before communion, before marriage, before 'extreme unction' and death, if the dying have sufficient strength for the task. And yet while this is undoubtedly the throne of priestly power in the Church, it is also the seat of spiritual weakness, because its remedies are not specific and satisfactory, and, indeed, cannot be."

With these remarks came the hour for breaking up our interview.

IX.

GREAT STRUGGLES AND FALSE REFUGES—FIRST COM-
MUNION—PENANCES—CONFIRMED BY BISHOP (NOW
CARDINAL) McCLOSKEY—IN THE ARMY—EXTREME
UNCTION — THE SCAPULAR — YEARNINGS FOR THE
PRIESTHOOD—CHARLATANISM—WOES UNUTTERABLE.

*Lo, thou trusteth in the staff of this broken reed, on Egypt ; whereon if
a man lean, it will go into his hand, and pierce it.—Isaiah.*

THE constant recurrence of an event so
greatly removes its novelty, that, particularly with children, it is apt to
become stale or uninteresting. Therefore, I had feared that our gatherings
would soon lose their interest for our children's
minds, and thus fail in accomplishing the good
I desired. But I was mistaken. The facts presented were not only unfolding the inner workings of a gigantic and wonderful religious
organization whose outer manifestations are
constantly before our eyes, but they also revealed
the influence of this organization upon the
spiritual life and conduct of those around us,
even of some who were prominent in our dis-

cussions. There was, of course, a special interest
in the development of my own experience. So
on meeting—and every one was promptly on
time—the general inquiry seemed to be as to
what power the doctrines and doings which I
had attempted to describe had exerted upon my
inner life, and I commenced.

" When I was very young, deep religious impressions were made upon my heart. At the
age of ten or twelve I was pungently convicted
of sin. Having read a little tract in French,
entitled ' *Eternité,*' an impression was received
which time never obliterated. For many weeks
after this my heart was sad, and every night
after retiring I spent hours in meditating upon
my sins, and my unpreparedness for eternity,
and often wept until my pillow was wet with
tears."

" But why did you not go to Jesus to beg his
pardon, as you have taught us to do ? " asked
Johnnie, weeping as he spoke.

" Simply because I had no one to direct me to
this sovereign remedy. But I was taught by
my mother to go and confess to the priest. This
I did in the most sincere, devout, and thorough
manner."

" Did you find the relief you desired ? " he
asked.

" I experienced a momentary relief when the

disagreeable task was done, accompanied with the vague and blind belief that all was right. But there would still arise the longing, ' O that I could know that my sins are indeed blotted out !' Had I possessed a thousand worlds I would cheerfully have consecrated them all to know, even for a single moment, that my sins were removed from me ' as far as the east is from the west.' But I was told that this is a great mystery which no human mind can comprehend, and that I must, therefore, leave it all to the power and good intentions of the priest. But the teachings of my intellect could not repress the yearnings of my heart. My soul was ' like the troubled sea,' when it cannot rest, ' whose waters cast up mire and dirt.' And as with ocean waves, ebbing and flowing, there was a perpetual moaning and oscillation between sighing and tears—a condition well expressed by the poet Montgomery :—

> " ' O where shall rest be found,—
> Rest for the weary soul ?
> 'Twere vain the ocean's depths to sound,
> Or pierce to either pole.'

" When I made my first communion—"

" O, what is that ? " interrupted Johnnie, rather abruptly.

" It is the first time one partakes of the holy communion. The child then is expected volun-

tarily to assume the vows taken by his sponsors,
or godfather and godmother, at the time of baptism.   The Catechism has first to be thoroughly
learned.   The Sabbath previous to the real communion, in order to prepare the candidates more
perfectly for that solemn event, all the children,
sufficiently versed in the Catechism, and supposed to be truly penitent, enjoy what they call
' *communion en blanc.*'   You can interpret it
either communion in white, or in blank, for it
is both.   The little girls are all dressed in white,
and the boys are neatly attired, while each is
garlanded with wreaths of flowers and evergreens.
After performing various ceremonies, at the
proper time they are led to the altar, and the
priest goes through the regular process of admin-
istering communion to them with unconsecrated,
that is, with 'blank' wafers.   The week following is generally spent in solemn devotions, such
as going frequently to confession, perhaps every,
day; spending many hours in church repeating
and reading prayers; fasting and performing
other penances, until the Sabbath arrives. Then
the services are made especially impressive, and
the occasion is long remembered.

"When I made my first communion I was as
truly penitent as it seems to me any one could
be.   It was not with me as I am sure it is with
many, who, as the day of confession approaches,

grow restless and gloomy, and who mistake the shame of their disgusting disclosure for the sincere repentance of their sins. For at least forty-eight hours I wept almost incessantly. My soul was in an agony of desire to be freed from its load of sin. I panted for freedom. I fasted till I well-nigh fainted. Sin! I hated it; I abhorred it. I hated myself, because I was a sinner. There was no penance I was not willing to perform; and I confidently expected help from the ordinances of God's house. But all my promises of reformation and my prayers, added to those of the priest and his absolution, were in vain. The fountain of my disease had not been reached. I was still a slave, sold under sin. I saw what seemed to be right, but failed to do it; I knew what was wrong, and yet did it. The temple of my soul was in ruins. My heart was the hold of every foul spirit, and a cage of every unclean and hateful bird and beast, each clamouring for the ascendency. My intellectual faculties had declared war against my moral nature, and my bodily infirmities and wants had taken up arms against both. There was a contradiction, a conflict within me."

"O, father!" exclaimed Luella, "how perfectly that condition is described in the seventh chapter of Paul's Epistle to the Romans." She then read from the fourteenth verse to nearly the close of the chapter, ending with the lamentation, " O, wretched man that I am ! who shall deliver me from the body of this death ?"

"Yes; that was the wail of my weary soul. But to my pitiful inquiry came back the sad, the only echo, 'Who?' There were inward cravings and yearnings which found no satisfaction in external rites. Indeed, these ceremonies only complicated and increased my difficulties. I found I had leaned upon a reed which not only broke, but whose splintered and jagged ends made a fearful wound in my spirit, for the healing of which I knew no balm."

"O!" exclaimed Monsieur Grenier, "why is it that I, in having a similar experience, should have thought that no one else ever had such trouble as myself ? You have described my own struggles of soul even better than I could have done."

"Few persons, if any," I replied, "have, as I have learned, a *unique* experience; and yet nearly every one is tempted to believe that no one can ever know his griefs and truly care for his soul. This, too, was a sore trial to me at the time. But I have not told you all I wish to. Other expedients to relieve my spiritual distresses were suggested, accompanied with greater fastings and more humiliating prayers. I was taught that confirmation—a sacrament which,

like baptism, can be received but once, and at
the hands of a bishop—would impart to me the
'Holy Ghost, and make me strong, and a perfect Christian and soldier of Jesus Christ.'
Bishop John McCloskey, then of the diocese of
Albany, now Cardinal at New York, was about
to visit Ticonderoga to administer this holy
sacrament. I looked forward to the occasion
with unusual interest. All due preparation of
heart and mind was made for the longed-for
day. By the parish priest, Mr. Olivetti, an
Italian, residing at Whitehall, N. Y. at whose
hand I had communed, I was regarded as having
made sufficient proficiency in the preceding
degree to entitle me to this, and with others I
was presented for this final seal of discipleship,
to be confirmed in the faith, and fortified
against all its visible and invisible enemies. My
soul breaking out with intense longing for
divine assistance, I stood before that august pre-
late, a splendid man to look upon, attired in his
episcopal robes; was anointed with the holy
chrism in the sign of the cross on my forehead,
and dismissed with the tap of his jewelled
finger on my cheek, accompanied with the
blessing, '*pax tecum*,' that is, peace be with
thee. Then I retired to test in real life the
blessing which they assured me was then given
to me. But, alas! alas! what were my sub-

sequent dismay and despair when I discovered that, like the woman spoken of in the gospels, 'I was nothing bettered, but rather grew worse.' I was not more wicked than before, but I felt more corruption within. With every increased effort to overcome sin I saw more and more vividly my sinfulness and helplessness. The chained or caged tiger when asleep or in quiet may seem as free as his fellows which rest in the deep jungles; but when he tugs at his chain, or lashes in vain the iron bars, he feels his bondage and weakness. So the 'law of sin and death' held me fast, and had I known the words, my cry would have been,—

> "'Nor bleeding bird, nor bleeding breast,
> Nor hyssop branch, nor sprinkling priest,
> Nor running brook, nor flood, nor sea,
> Can wash the dismal stain away.'

"My state was deplorable beyond description. Often when alone — and I greatly courted solitude, and many times contemplated the life of a hermit, such as I had read of in the history of the so-called saints of the Middle Ages—I was so consumed by my inward griefs and filled with unutterable agony, that I would often cease from work, if employed, and stand for many minutes like a mute, cold statue. And yet I was at times extremely gay in society, where I sought to drown my hidden woes. No one of my acquaintances was more social and vivacious than myself, and I was often the leader in games, sports, and tricks, sometimes spending whole nights in convivialities. But more than once in the midst of a game at cards, or in the figures of a dance, or in a lively chit-chat with friends, I was siezed with a strange conviction of my sinfulness that I was scarcely able to hide from those around me. When I was alone, I sighed for something I could not find. I was an enigma to myself, filled with the extremes of gaiety and griefs, of sunshine and shade, with a tincture of soul-bitterness diffused through the whole.

"At times my nature seemed to be an ugly conglomeration of hyena teeth and wasp stings, of serpent scales and porcupine quills, thoroughly sprinkled with fire and brimstone, for I had a terribly high temper, which, when aroused, was fearful and cruel; and yet I was capable of the most delicate appreciation of the beautiful in nature and in morals, and my heart was open to the tenderest sympathies. The war-like, poetic, and religious spirit of my ancestors had in me a strange blending. Some days I was woefully wicked, and yet my conscience was so tender that if through haste, in the morning, I happened to perform any ordinary labour before offering my prayer; or if I failed to give due attention to the prayer—though every one will

easily see the difficulty of repeating every day
from memory a prayer in an unknown tongue
without wanderings of thought; or if, by
mistake, I chanced even to taste meat on
Friday, or was guilty of any similiar delin-
quency, I was thrown into a kind of spiritual
convulsion, from which I could not recover until
I had confessed it all to the priest, and performed my penance. All this was far from
relieving me; but when the old score was can-
celled, I seemed to run into other spiritual debts
with a somewhat lighter heart. I might have
applied to myself, with a good degree of appro-
priateness, the quaint old couplet—

" ' To good and evil equal bent,
      I'm both a devil and a saint.'

And thus in grief my days passed wearily by.
my soul muttering constantly the sentiments of
a few lines in Lee's Mithridates, which I afterward found :—

" ' What miracle
Can work me into hope ?   Heaven here is bankrupt :
The wondering gods blush at their want of power,
And, quite abashed, confess they cannot help me !' "

"I can scarcely comprehend," said the Professor, who had not yet spoken a word, "how
you could endure such constant grief without
breaking down your constitution."

"I ought to mention, to the praise of God,

that he gave me a constitution endowed with rare powers of endurance. For upwards of thirty years I have not been detained from the labours of my vocation a single half day, nor confined to the house one hour by illness. This is true, though two and a half of those years were spent in the trying campaigns of the armies of the Potomac, and of the Shenandoah, including three months' confinement in Libby Prison, in the midst of starvation, filthiness, and death. To pains and aches, however, I am comparatively a stranger. But I ought to mention as a reason for this physical soundness and strength, that from childhood I have strictly adhered to a total abstinence pledge, and have never made use of tobacco in any form. I have made the ' laws of health ' a subject of study and practice. And I believe that the teaching of these principles — so frequently urged in the Bible— especially to the young, is a great want of the times. Excuse me, if you please, for this digression.

" But to my spiritual griefs there were also given intervals of comparative rest, though, like angels' visits, they were ' few and far between.' My principal relief was found in religious devotions. So I increased my fastings and prayers. I had frequent resource to the Virgin Mary and to my patron saint. I often visited the Church, and went through the *via crucis,* or way of the cross, making prayers at the different stations in the Passion of our Lord, represented by the images on the walls, dolefully dragging myself on my knees around the entire church.   I repeated my confessions to the priest and received the communion, but these I found to my great grief availed me even less than at first, for they became more mechanical, less earnest and real."

"I should think," said Luella, "that you would have become discouraged and given up all hope."

"I certainly should, had not other refuges been presented.   I was taught to expect assistance in 'extreme unction' and 'purgatory.' But these were future, and hence not wholly satisfactory.   The promise of food next week does not satisfy the hunger of to-day; and it avails nothing at all, unless you have ground to hope that you will hold out until the expected relief arrives.   But here was my perplexity.   I was taught that extreme unction is a holy sacrament which imparts spiritual succour to the sick and dying, and that no one receiving it can possibly be lost."

"Is it not substantially the teaching of St. James?" asked Nora.

"Not at all, Nora, as I understand the passage.

St. James recommends the oil to be used medi-
cinally, as is the practice in those eastern lands
even to this day. The good Samaritan poured
oil in the wounds of the afflicted man. It was
evidently the prayer of faith, as St. James tells
us, that should raise the sick, if a miraculous
raising was effected. The oil was only a
natural remedy, and the effect was natural. But
the priests of the Romish Church use it, not
with the intention of raising the sick—for they
never administer it when there is even a prospect
of recovery—but by some magical influence to
prepare the sick to die. This is not the intent
of St. James. The administration of extreme
unction in Canada is made a season of great
solemnity. I have several times assisted the
priest in this holy office. He, carrying the
consecrated wafer in its golden pyx, marches
solemnly from the church to the house of the
dying, accompanied by a few acolytes, one of
whom, or the sexton, preceding him some distance, rings a hand-bell, the peculiar sound of
which is readily understood by all who hear it, to
announce that ' *le bon Dieu*,' the good God, even
our Lord Jesus Christ himself, is about to pass
by. Everybody thus forewarned, is ready as the
priest comes, to kneel down, either in the street,
or in the house, or shop, or field, and with bowed
head to worship the passing deity."

"But," exclaimed Johnnie, "how is it that we never see any such procession in this country?"

"Simply because in these parts they carry the wafer god more privately," Aunt Melie replied.

"To prevent scandal," added Nora, "where there are so many Protestant unbelievers."

"I cannot see," said Luella, "how anything scriptural, anything which ought to be done for the dying could be scandalous."

Nora seemed to feel the force of the remark, and remained thoughtfully silent, while I went on:—

"The priest, having reached the place, orders tapers or candles to be lighted, repeats many prayers and litanies, and then making three times the sign of the cross upon the sick one at the name of each person of the Trinity, says, 'In the name of the Father, and of the Son, and of the Holy Ghost, may all power of the devil be extinguished in thee by the laying on of our hands, and the invocation of all the holy angels, archangels, patriarchs, prophets, apostles, martyrs, confessors, virgins, and all the saints.' Then dipping his thumb in the chrism, he anoints the sick person in the form of the cross upon the eyes, ears, nose, mouth, hands, and feet; at each anointing making use of this form of prayer: 'Through this holy unction, and His own most tender mercy, may the Lord pardon thee whatever sin thou hast committed by thy sight. Amen.' And so of the hearing, and of the rest, adapting the form to the several senses." *

"I should think that would be enough to kill even a well person!" added Aunt Melie.

"But the impression made upon my mind was, that so imposing a ceremony must be quite efficacious to prepare the soul for its exit from earth; and so I was taught. I knew that only a priest could administer this sacrament, and that when any one was sick we always sent for him sooner than for the physician. This inspired in me such strong yearnings toward the priesthood, that I resolved either to become a priest myself, or to be somewhat associated with one, so that I could not fail to secure his services in the dying hour. This desire was intensified by hearing my father pray during Lent—the only time we had family worship—that God would save us from sudden death. But my father was too poor to afford to educate me for a priest, or even to spare me to be the servant of one. Here was another serious obstacle to my salvation. These untoward circumstances caused me no little uneasiness.

"But right in the midst of these perplexities

* Challoner's "Catholic Instructed," p. 111.

11

it seemed as if Providence smiled on me. A mission, or what we would call 'a series of extra meetings,' was held in our town, under the direction and labours of Brothers Telmon, Lagier, and others, known as the Oblate missionaries; and during these meetings they presented the saving and miraculous influences of the *scapular*."

At the mention of this word, the Professor, who sat near the table, took the dictionary, and finding the place, read : " A part of the habit of certain religious orders in the Roman Catholic Church, consisting of two bands of woollen stuff worn over the gown, of which one crosses the back or shoulder, and the other the stomach. This is worn as a badge of peculiar veneration for the Virgin Mary."

When he had closed the book I said : " But as this mode of wearing the scapular would not be convenient for labouring people, those ' brothers ' directed us to make them of two small pieces of woollen stuff two or three inches square, but double, so as to form a receptacle for medals of the Virgin, or relics of some old saint, or an *agnus Dei*, which is a cake of wax stamped with the figure of a lamb supporting the banner of the cross, blessed by the Pope with solemn prayer, and anointed with holy chrism. This, too, is supposed to possess the power of preserving those who carry it in faith, from accidents and sudden death. These two double pieces of cloth, fastened together by two strings or ribbons which pass on either side of the neck, were to be worn next the body, one on the breast, the other on the back."

Here I unlocked a little box and exhibited to the company a scapular, which Mrs. Beaudry had made for this occasion.

"Why!" exclaimed Johnnie, "it is just like what I saw on several boys last summer, when we went into the river bathing. They tied them fast around their necks, ' for fear of losing them,' they said. And when I asked what they were, and why they did not take them off and leave them with their clothes, they blushed, but would not tell me."

While he was talking, Nora quickly disappeared from the room, but soon returning with a scapular in one hand and an *agnus Dei* in the other, she gave the former to Johnnie and the latter to Mary, observing :—" There ; I have been fooled long enough ! For nearly five years I have been wearing these trinkets and trusting in them, instead of trusting in the only Lamb of God. You may have them as momentoes of my former ignorance, or for playthings." This brief speech had an electrical effect on every one. When quiet was restored, I further explained :—

" We were told that this thing originated with Simon Stock, general of the Carmelites, an order of monks. The celebrated Pére Hyacinthe, now one of the leaders of the 'Old Catholic' party in Europe, formerly belonged to this order. It was said that while this Simon was engaged in devotions on or about July 16th, 1251, the Virgin Mary appeared to him."

" Times must have changed since Gospel days," interrupted Luella, with a play of irony in her manner, " for I read that Jesus then appeared to Simon, but I have never read in the Bible that the Virgin Mary after death ever appeared to any of the sacred writers."

" I am giving you the authority of the Roman Catholic Church now. Please keep this in mind. As the account went, the Virgin had a scapular in her hands, which she placed upon the devout monk, and assured him that whoever should wear a similar one in her honour, and daily repeat an *Ave Maria* and *Pater noster* should not die in mortal sin—that is, without the succours of the priesthood. We were further told that the thing had never failed to afford the promised relief, numberless miracles of preservation from death on land and sea being cited to prove the efficacy of the great revelation, and to stimulate the faith of the people.

" This was just the thing I wanted. At the
close of the service, during which I had listened
with rapt attention to these wonderful disclosures, I ran home to relate what I had heard
to my mother, who had remained busy with
her work, for we were carrying on a brisk trade
in eatables and home-made beer with the multitudes who were attracted to these meetings
from all the 'region round about.' I quickly
described to her the scapular, and soon the
whole family, who appeared quite as much
interested as myself, was supplied with these
holy life-preservers, and ready to be received
into the order. The day was appointed for the
solemn service of inauguration, and thousands
came together of old and young, each bringing
his new-made scapular with him. Some were
beautifully wrought in the highest style of
needlework, while others were very plain. At
the hour appointed, the multitudes crowded to
the altar where we knelt, one priest blessing
the scapulars with holy water, and another
putting them on our necks, amid chanting of
hymns to the Virgin Mary, who was believed to
have vouchsafed to her children so distinguished
a mark of her love and power. A prayer was
also offered in which we promised to take the
Virgin for our Patroness, our Advocate, and our

Mother, pledged ourselves to be her children and perpetual servants, and ended in saying to her, "Grant, by thy powerful intercession, that I may have a perfect zeal for thy honour, and that this holy scapular, which I desire to carry during my whole life as a witness of my dedication to thee, may be the means of preserving me from the dangers of eternal death, and conducting me in safety to everlasting bliss. Amen.'" *

"O, what doubly-compounded idolatry!" cried Aunt Melie. "And was there no fear of quackery in your mind? A quack, you know, always professes either to cure all kinds of diseases with one medicine, or to cure one specific disease with a great variety of medicines. Now, the Gospel, as I understand it, recognizes but one great disease in humanity, namely, sin. It proposes but one remedy, and that one specific and sovereign, namely, the blood of Jesus Christ. But according to the facts you have stated—and I cannot think I have forgotten one of them—you were made to depend for the pardon of sin and salvation upon a great variety of things. I may not be able to give the doses in their proper order, but here is the general prescription: 1. Baptism; 2. Sacrament of penance, or confession to a priest; 3. Penances performed by yourself;

* "Way to Heaven," p. 391.

4. Communion; 5. Confirmation; 6. Extreme unction; 7. Holy water; 8. Holy chrism; 9. Palm branches; 10. Crucifixes; 11. Way-side crosses; 12. Images; 13. The Virgin Mary; 14. Other saints; 15. Angels; 16. Relics; 17. Medals; 18. *Agnus Dei;* 19. Scapulars; 20. Rosary chaplets; 21. Pilgrimages; 22. Masses; 23. Indulgences; 24. Purgatory! If this be not a perfect specimen of religious quackery, pray tell me what it is?"

"I assure you that I did not then see it in that light. I was taught to regard this great variety of expedients as an evidence of the unlimited bounty of the Church, showing her inventive genius and marvellous power."

"But could you not see that, if any one of these two dozen things had been a truly divine, and hence all-sufficient remedy, no other would have been sought after? No one would be so foolish as to call a second physician, if the first were all-wise and all-powerful to relieve!"

" O, I did not stop to reason much upon the subject, for the Church told me not to do so. I was only perplexed to know which expedient was most salutary; and I hoped that in the great multitude of them, some one, or the joint influence of them all, would, perhaps, somehow and somewhere, prove satisfactory.

"But I had a wonderful confidence in my scapular. I never, for a single moment, removed it from my body for fear of dying without it. When the first became old, and the strings began to give way, I had another made, but the new one was put on before the old was displaced. I then actually believed my scapular saved my life on several occasions—once from the kick of a horse, which just grazed my face, and once from the fall of a tree, which barely missed my head."

"How much like my own, thus far, your experience has been," interrupted Monsieur Grenier; "but how did you feel at last?"

"Wretchedly unhappy. For with all my helps in priests and prayers, I was still conscious of dark depravity within. I loathed myself, and found no rest for my soul. I was like one pursuing a splendid mirage or phantom. I was only repeating my childhood sports, though sadly, when for hours of sunshine through the meadows I chased the gaudy butterfly, or at eventide the star-like firefly, without catching them ; or by moonlight endeavoured to overleap my own shadow, which, with equal pace, fled as I advanced. It was the old story of Tantalus, whom Ulysses was fabled to have seen in the lower world, standing up to his chin in water, which constantly eluded his lip as often as he attempted to quench the thirst that tormented him. Over his head grew all kinds of fruits; but whenever he reached forth his hands to pluck them, the wind scattered them to the clouds. I think that Isaiah has most graphically described my state. He says: 'It shall even be as when a hungry man dreameth, and, behold, he eateth; but he awaketh, and his soul is empty: or as when a thirsty man dreameth, and, behold, he drinketh; but he awaketh, and, behold, he is faint.'

"I looked upon the singing birds and the grazing cattle with envy. O! why had I power to know right and wrong, when I had not power to follow the former nor to overcome the latter? Why had I a conscience to scourge me as with scorpions? I could have cried,—

> "'O that I had been formed
> An idiot from the birth! a senseless changeling,
> Who eats his gluttons' meals with greedy haste,
> Nor knows the hand which feeds him!'

I would have gladly exchanged existence even with a loathsome, crawling viper. I could never account for such a dreadful thought; it must have been purely Satanic. Life was to me a bitter thing, and death I looked upon with shrinking horror. In my deep distress I cursed the day that gave me being, and wished that I had died in my childhood. Terrible as is the desire, I prayed for annihilation! I arraigned the God of heaven, and came near cursing my Maker. These struggles oontinued for several years. Certain passages in the penitential psalms perfectly expressed my state:—

"'I am weary with my groaning; all the night make I my bed to swim; I water my couch with my tears. For my iniquities are gone over mine head: as a heavy burden they are too heavy for me. For my days are consumed like smoke, and my bones are burned as a hearth. My heart is smitten and withered like grass; so that I forget to eat my bread. By reason of the voice of my groaning my bones cleave to my skin. I am like a pelican of the wilderness; I am like the owl of the desert. I watch, and am as a sparrow alone upon the housetop.'"

With this sad portraiture of my state before us we were compelled to close our interview, for swift-winged Time announced the call to other duties.

X.

PROVIDENTIAL MEANS OF RELIEF—TICONDEROGA—
LEAVING HOME—CREAM HILL, VT.—AT SCHOOL—
GREAT PROGRESS—TEACHING—HENRYVILLE, CANADA
—DIARY—JOSEPH COOK—EXTEMPORE SPEAKING.

I will bring the blind by a way that they knew not; I will lead them in paths they have not known; I will make darkness light before them, and crooked things straight.—Isaiah.

MANY moments of the week which followed our last conversation were spent in studying the interesting cartoons in "Harper's Weekly," with which the children, and especially Nora, who was personally acquainted with some of the parties represented, were perfectly delighted. By placing several successive numbers of this brilliant periodical on a long table, side by side, we could readily trace the history of the revelations of the most astounding official corruption of modern times, accompanied with priestly interference with our system of common, schools, and intermeddling with politics. These papers greatly increased the interest in my story, while they revived memories of events and principles already explained.

On assembling this time we missed our friend, Monsieur Grenier; but the Professor was promptly on hand—indeed he had accompanied us from the Sunday-school. Luella had not forgotten the gloomy description of my state of mind, given last Sabbath, and as soon as possible she said:—

"Now, father, pray tell us in what way you were ever led to abandon the views you formerly entertained, and how you came in possession of the cheerful, spiritual frame of mind in which I have always known you to be."

"It affords me great pleasure, I assure you, to be able to turn from that shady side of my life to one more sunny; from that midnight gloom to the bright, glowing day. But the story is not a very brief one."

"Never mind the length," almost shouted Johnnie, "so long as it is good. When we little folks begin to get weary, it will probably be time to stop; but I hope not before."

"With this assurance on your part I will proceed. But I wish to preface my narrative by saying, that the leadings of Providence are often very mysterious and surprising. Cowper wrote:—

"'God moves in a mysterious way,
His wonders to perform.'

In view of this great truth, Jeremiah exclaims, ' O Lord, I know that the way of man is not in himself : it is not in man that walketh to direct his steps.' The history of Abraham, the father and type of true believers, beautifully exemplifies the same truth. God's hand may be seen also in all the wanderings of the Hebrew people. We see it especially in the history of Saul of Tarsus, afterwards the Apostle Paul. How little did he know, when he left Jerusalem with letters from the chief priests, authorizing him to destroy, by every means possible, the newly-rising sect of Nazarenes, that in a few days he would be preaching the faith he was then so zealously endeavouring to overthrow ; consorting with the very people against whom he was breathing out threatening and slaughter ; building up the Church of which he was making so fearful a havoc, and suffering persecution at the hands of his nation and family ! God led him in a way he knew not, and took the scales of error from his eyes. In after years he wrote to Timothy concerning himself in these humiliating terms : ' Who was before a blasphemer, and a persecutor, and injurious ; but I obtained mercy because I did it ignorantly in unbelief.' In more· respects than one the same· statement is true of myself."

"Was your conversion, indeed, like St. Paul's?' inquired Luella.

"In many respects the conversion of every Christian resembles his, and it was particularly so with mine, as you will see at the proper time in my narrative. But now I want to tell you of the providential means that led to so important an event. Leaving home is the first thing I will mention. Sad as I felt at the time, this was, nevertheless, a God-send, I am sure.

"On March 3, 1848, my father died. As he left no property for the children to trust in or to quarrel over, each one had to go forth and 'paddle his own canoe.' My father's death occurred in a wild region called New Hague, on the southern border of the town of Ticonderoga, about two miles from Lake George. An older brother had purchased a farm there, and, with hired men, set to work to clear the land and bring it into cultivation. As I was a stout boy for one of my age, I was also hired with other brothers. At this hard work I spent more than a year. But while the land was being cleared and cultivated, my heart and mind were not only neglected, but brought under the grossest influences. The morals of the place were utterly wretched. There was neither school-house nor church for several miles. The region was a rendezvous of second-rate lumbermen, worn out 'canallers,' and runaways from justice, with very few exceptions. Dancing and drinking, with all manner of vulgarities and obscenities, were the order of the day. The Sabbaths were occasions of the most rampant wickedness; except once in four weeks, when the whole neighbourhood disgorged the majority of its population, who went several miles to the Roman Catholic Church in Ticonderoga. It was during this period that I passed through some of the most fearful experiences of my life. Most corrupt practices were there taught me, and yet at times I struggled, though in vain, to shake off the monster that was devouring my very vitals. It was at this time, however, that I got acquainted with Joseph Cook, who proved to be my deliverer.

"In the autumn of 1849, through a little misunderstanding, I was drawn into a sharp encounter of words with my brother, for whom I was working. This led to our separation, and to my leaving home. Too late he repented, and confessed his undeserved rebuke of me, and strove to retain me; but I was determined, and would not stay. You have read of Benjamin Franklin, whom difficulties with a brother sent out into the world, and who went to Philadelphia, with three rolls of bread under his arm, and his pockets stuffed with stockings and shirts —these being all the estate he possessed. Well, it was something such an appearance I presented as I took my little bundles and started out to seek my fortune. My mother piously commended me to the Virgin Mary, and told me not to forget my Church, nor my scapular. I embraced her, shedding tears which I endeavoured in vain to restrain, and left."

" But why did you cry so ? " inquired Johnnie, almost sobbing as he said it.

" O, I can scarcely tell you why. But the world looked so cold and wide, and I was going forth into it penniless, friendless—a wretched, ignorant boy. Then, too, I had so strong an attachment to my friends, especially to my dear mother, that this separation nearly broke my heart. I moved away from the house with slow, measured steps, and as I went over the first knoll, whence I could take a last look of home, I turned and saw my mother still standing at the door with her apron to her face. Had it not been for what seemed the leadings of an invisible hand, which some, I suppose, would call the hand of Destiny, I could not have gone farther. But the die was cast; the Rubicon was crossed; so I resumed my journey. I had a brother living in a place called Cream Hill—a name of good omen—in the town of Shoreham, Addison County, Vermont. Thither I bent my steps. After spending a weary and almost sleepless night with my brother, I found a good place with a neighboring farmer named Perry, who needed just such help as I could render.

"My mother had carefully taught me how to mend my clothes and darn my stockings, and I now found a good opportunity to practise what I had learned. She had also urged me to go to school, if I could possibly find a suitable place. It had been her misfortune as well as my father's to be without education. Hence their mark (X) instead of their name may be found in several documents. To gratify her as well as myself, I sought a place with diligence, and succeeded."

"This leads me to speak of another powerful means which God made use of in bringing about my conversion, namely, education. Having laboured for Mr. William E. Perry until his fall work was finished, I went to Mr. Hiram Rich, who resided near the school-house, agreeing to do 'chores,' which consisted mostly in feeding five or six hundred sheep, and some cattle, for which labour I was to be boarded. As his daughter was the school teacher and boarded at home, I was to receive her assistance in my lessons, especially evenings—an arrangement which proved highly beneficial.

"I was then sixteen years old, large of my age, and yet I could scarcely read or write, and was ignorant of the elementary rules or principles of arithmetic. I was not a little ashamed of myself as I appeared among my fellow-pupils, most of whom were much younger than I in years, and yet several years my superiors in knowledge. My French pride was terribly wounded, but it seemed to urge me on in my efforts, and I began to apply myself night and day. I soon became so absorbed in my books that I could think of little else. Sometimes I was even forgetful of my work. But Mr. Rich would kindly excuse me by saying, 'I know what's the matter with you: your studies fill your entire mind.' It was no uncommon thing for me to solve some of the most difficult problems of my arithmetic in my dreams. I often studied during recesses when others were at play. In fact, I studied everywhere, and all the time. It seemed as if every power of my intellect—and I had reached a period of life when the mind is peculiarly active—was focalized upon improvement. This was the charmed circle around which all my thoughts revolved and within which they were centréd. As even a few solar rays, caught by a convex lens, converge to a burning point, so this harmony and unity of my mental powers produced an intense eagerness for knowledge, supplied me with light as I advanced, and dispelled or dissolved the difficulties that obstructed my way. I have learned that it is application and enthusiasm, more than great opportunities or talents, that accomplish any work."

"This is the key of success," said the Professor. "But, pray, give us the particulars of your achievements."

"My progress astonished both myself and others. In three months' time I had gone through what was called ' Adams's New Arithmetic,' so that there was not a problem in it I could not solve, and scarcely a principle I could not explain. Then, for the first time, I took up grammar and philosophy, finding in both the keenest enjoyment. This unlooked-for success changed the whole tenor of my life. Friends began to advise me to pursue a regular course of study. My mother, wonderfully gratified at my success, urged me to press on in this direction. There was one notable obstacle in my path, however. I was entirely destitute of means, and too proud to ask friends for help. But I had a vigorous frame, and was not afraid nor ashamed to work; and I saw how my hands and feet might be made to contribute to my brain. So when the winter term closed I engaged to work again for Mr. Perry, and the proceeds of my summer's work were sufficient to enable me to attend most of the fall term at Newton Academy, in the village of Shoreham. At the close of the term I received from the principal,

Mr. Asa S. Jones, a very gratifying recommendation for the position of district school teacher.

"I then presented myself to the school superintendent of the town of Ticonderoga, and after a rigid examination, received a legal certificate which bears date November 12, 1850. But it was too late in the season ; I found that the schools were either commenced or had their teachers engaged. However, as I was only seventeen years of age, and, perhaps, too young to have succeeded in teaching, I considered that it was all for the best that I failed in my efforts, and so returned to Cream Hill to attend the district school, as I did the winter before. The next spring my brother, who had been the cause of my leaving home, urged me so strongly to return and work for him that I consented, and spent the summer labouring at house-carpentry.

"In the autumn of 1851, I secured a school in the town of Hague, Warren County, N.Y., where I succeeded so well that, after teaching three months, I was re-engaged for a fourth. Then, taking my newly-earned money, I hastened to Henryville, Canada, where, for the sake of perfecting myself in my vernacular, I spent most of the season in a French school. While there, I was more deeply impressed than ever with the contrast between Protestant and Roman Catholic morality. I lamented to find it so, and was anxious to discover some power that could put a stop to the violations of the Sabbath; and I yearned to be able to do something myself for the moral elevation of my fellow-religionists. I sometimes wept over the moral desolation that prevailed. But in private conversation with intimate friends, especially with my eldest sister, in whose family I boarded, I found that the state of things was quite comfortably acquiesced in, because tolerated by the Church authorities, or, at least, tacitly sanctioned. Notwithstanding my perplexities with regard to such licensed irregularities, I went to confession to the priest, Rev. Mr. St. Aubain, and partook of the holy communion. By him, and by means of certain books put into my hands, I was taught to feel that all my troubles on this score were temptations of Satan; that the delinquencies of Church-members were no argument against the purity of the Church, and that somehow the Church, by means of her indulgences and spiritual authority, could remove these blotches. So instead of losing confidence in the Roman Catholic Church, I was forced into a greater admiration of an institution that could accomplish so great a thing.

"Strongly confirmed in these views, I returned to the States, and continued to prosecute my education, teaching winters, and attending school summers, except that through haying and harvest time I generally felt compelled to labour with my hands, for the sake of the increased wages. After being in school, either as a teacher or pupil, for about nine months in succession, my hands were tender and my frame relaxed, so that the result of the first few days of toil was worse than I can describe. I have had these hands so completely blistered, and my body so overstrained, that I have found myself in the morning so stiffened and sore as scarcely to be able to move, or to handle a tool. But the ultimate object stimulated me, and I endured 'hardness as a good soldier.' I know what hard work is, and, when inured to it, I loved it for its own sake. But sometimes I murmured at my lot, and envied those fellow-students whose parents gave them money to supply all their wants, while I was compelled to deny myself fine clothes, many needed books, and all delicacies. But it was all right. I cau see it now. I needed the discipline. It threw me upon my own resources, and gave me a better appreciation of what I gained. I dearly learned, that self-denial leads to self-control, and that these make self-reliance possible.

"In the autumn of 1852 I began to write a

diary or journal, which I have ever since continued."

"Do you mean this pile of books on the shelf?" asked Johnnie; and so speaking, he took out the seventeen volumes which are written, being about all he could lift. "And are all these books written through?" he continued. "I would like to know how many pages there are." The number of pages in each book was pencilled down by Luella as he called them off, which, with the volume I am now writing, amounted to nearly four thousand pages.

"It is not the number of pages I care much about, children, but it is the improvement I made in writing them. These pages, with the composition or themes I used to write almost weekly, greatly stimulated my thinking powers."

"I am sure," added the Professor, "that the practice of writing such a diary not only preserves many important events and incidents which might otherwise be lost, but greatly increases the power and facility with which a writer can produce narrative or history. It also teaches how to think deliberately and correctly."

"Thank you, Professor. I hope your remark may stimulate my children in the habit of journal-writing," I replied.

"About the time I commenced this practice, which, as you may see in volume first, was September 11, 1852, I also commenced the exercise of speaking extempore. With my school-mate, Joseph Cook, of Ticonderoga—who is now a Congregational minister of Boston, justly celebrated for his popular lectures— whose portrait you see on the wall, I agreed upon the following plan: We wrote subjects upon small pieces of paper, folded them, and put them into a hat. After shaking them thoroughly, we took turns in drawing out a slip, and in speaking off-hand upon whatever topic was written on it. This practice, persevered in, taught us to think rapidly and on our feet. Without the habit of close study and careful writing, however, this ability would have been hurtful; but now it proved to be a great help. Such was the improvement we obtained in this way, that we organized a literary society, which had extemporaneous speaking as its chief object, called it the 'Keeseville Cabal,' and gathered into it the best students of the academy we were attending besides several young men of the village. The attention I paid to the study of the Greek Latin, Spanish, and German languages also aided me to a better understanding of the English and French tongues, and served to discipline my mind. Some of these studies were of incalculable importance to me in subsequent investigations of religious truths."

"But what had education to do in bringing you to Christ?" asked Aunt Melie.

"Much every way. It gave me a key with which to unlock the difficult problems that presented themselves before me, while it intensified my desire to know the truth of every doctrine commended to my faith and practice. It also enlarged and liberalized my views of religion, of men, and of things in general. 'My people perish for want of knowledge,' said God by the mouth of an ancient prophet, and current history confirms such a statement. Education is a mighty power, reminding one of the mystic lever of Archimedes, who is reported to have said to King Hiero, 'Give me where I may stand, and I will move the world.' Assume education to be this lever, the Bible the fulcrum, and experimental and practical Christianity the hand on the long arm of the lever, and you have a force that cannot fail to lift the masses upward."

"A liberal education, free from all sectarianism, I am convinced, is not only the hope of Christianity, but also of all republics," added the Professor.

"I know," I said, "that religion without culture leads to bigotry. Zeal without knowledge results in shameful excesses. Witness all religious wars or persecutions. On the other hand, knowledge—I will not say education, for this means the harmonious development of all the faculties—knowledge without religion generally leads to infidelity. Much learning, without God, makes men mad. We must blend the two. They are like the wings of a bird, which are both needed for its flight. In the language of my friend Cook, though applied to moral suasion and legal power in the temperance work, I may say of knowledge and religion, that 'whenever we have tried to move on one wing, our flight has been a sorry spiral. It is not claimed that either wing is yet fledged to the full. But there is now historic ground to hope that, when both pinions are grown and both used in equal librations, the reform, as an archangel flying with steady vans in mid-heaven above the nations, and dispensing blessings, is to make the circuit of the globe.' Therefore, taking the word 'wisdom' for true religion, and 'understanding' for general education, I would urge these striking scriptural proverbs: 'Wisdom is the principal thing; therefore get wisdom : and with all thy getting, get understanding. Exalt her, and she shall promote thee; she shall bring thee to honour, when thou dost embrace her. She shall give to thine head an ornament of grace; a crown of glory shall she deliver to thee. Her ways are ways of pleasantness, and all her paths are peace.'"

With these golden utterances for each one to remember, our interview ended.

XI.

Persecution and Perplexity — Poor Nora — The Nuns — With Joseph Cook — Keeseville, N. Y. — First Hearing of the Word—Day Dawn—Sunday-School.

Ye have taken away my gods which I made, and the priest, and ye are gone away: and what have I more?—Micah, of Mount Ephraim.

THE interest in our interviews was becoming unaccountably enthusiastic. Indeed, scarcely a day passed that something in relation to them was not said. Nora, by her recent and peculiar experience, had become a centre of attraction, and bid fair to be a moving spirit among us. She was constantly receiving very severe letters from her father, who threatened to disown her if she did not leave us, and cast off "those Protestant heresies," as he expressed himself. Her mother maintained a more loving yet sorrowful attitude. At last she received a note from the priest, full of warnings, couched in such singular and equivocal terms, that two or three various interpretations could be attached to them. However, it was plain to see that the priest in whose parochial limits we resided had been pretty well informed of Nora's whereabouts; and it was quite clearly intimated that if she did not leave willingly, forcible measures might be instituted for that purpose. At first, Nora displayed some restlessness, and the fear of abduction tormented her. She had recently read Rev. Dr. Hiram Mattison's brief account of the kidnapping of Miss Mary Ann Smith, of Newark, New Jersey, who, for renouncing Romanism, and joining the Methodist Episcopal Church, and for no other cause, was forcibly abducted and incarcerated in the House of the Good Shepherd, one of those institutions in New York which are suckled at the breast of the public treasury. On reading the book she doubted its truthfulness, but now successive flashes of conviction that such treatment was possible, even for herself, made her feel uneasy. For some time her mind oscillated between doubt and fear. But one day she said to me, "If that's the way they expect to rule me, they will find themselves mistaken. What kind of religion can this be that would force obedience to its commands? That may have done well enough in old Ireland, but it will never do in free America. You know that this is my native land, and somehow, within the past few weeks particularly, it seems to me as if I was

strangely influenced by its free air and free
institutions, especially when I compare our
privileges with the condition of things in the
old country, as related to me by my parents.
Now, really, I can't believe that they mean to do
as is intimated in this letter. It must be it
means something else." And thus she continued
talking about the matter, endeavouring to
believe better things of her mother's church.
But that she had fears was evidenced by her
carrying the strange letter constantly in her
pocket and often reading it.

One evening, as she was returning from church
with Luella—for she had become greatly interested in our public meetings also—they met two
nuns, or "sisters," who on approaching them
gave signs of desiring to speak to them; but as
they chanced to meet in a strong lamp-light,
and near an alley, the nuns very ingeniously
stepped aside into the shade of the corner building,
and invited the girls to follow. The latter were
not a little startled at first on seeing the two
white bonnets flopping in the night wind, and
on being thus accosted; but as it was early in
the night, and the nuns appeared very pleasant,
they obeyed. On reaching the shaded nook, one
of them stepped up to Luella, and, in an under-
tone, inquired if she could tell her where the
Rev. Mr. Beaudry resided, in whose family lived

an Irish girl by the name of Nora O'C——. Nora, already suspicious of the strangers, on hearing her name thus called, instantly caught Luella by the hand, and unceremoniously and rapidly they both hastened home. They were so overcome with fear, and so nearly breathless from their chase when they arrived, that it was some time before they could recount the incident. Nora was so excited that locking and bolting the doors and windows would not quiet her, and I was induced to go out and engage a special policeman to watch the premises through the night. Under these circumstances, it was for some days difficult to tell what the poor girl would do. She was more or less nervous day and night, and did not dare on any account to enter the streets except in the daytime, and with some member of the family. I suggested the propriety of sending her to my brother Charles, near Lake Champlain, where, for some time at least, she might live in seclusion. But she averred that the priest knew all about him also, as he had declared to her in her last confession, so that that home would be no covert from his designs. And furthermore, she said she would regard such a flight as little less than downright cowardice.

At last her naturally independent Irish character began to assert its power. She was

greatly stimulated and directed by the evangelical truths which she had already treasured up,
and soon, with a spirit resembling that of Joan
of Arc, she resolved to brave and overcome the
fiercest dangers. She asserted that this "vic-
torious state of mind," as she called it, was
gained while engaged in prayer to her blessed
Saviour; and she meant now, if necessary, to
lose even her life for His sake. Her heroism was
really grand, and at times sublime, partaking
much of natural, though more of moral, courage.

In our first interview after this significant
event, when our whole company was present,
Nora elicited general sympathy, and several plans
were suggested to secrete her among our friends,
or by some means to make at least her liberty
of person secure. But avowing her purpose of
remaining with us and of trusting God for the
result, she finally relieved our anxiety by saying
that she had recently found a precious passage
in the prophecy of Isaiah, which she quoted as
follows: "No weapon that is formed against
thee shall prosper; and every tongue that shall
rise against thee in judgment thou shalt condemn.
This is the heritage of the servants of the Lord,
and their righteousness is of Me, saith the Lord."
"And then," she added, "if it comes to the
worst, Jesus has said, 'Fear not them which kill
the body, but are not able to kill the soul: but

rather fear Him which is able to destroy both soul and body in hell.' I'll risk my destiny, then, in the hands of Him who has all power in heaven and in earth."

Johnnie, who was sitting near me, whispered in my ear, "Don't you think, father, that Nora is truly converted? It seems almost as though her face was shining like an angel's."

"Let us have no privacies here," I whispered back; "Nora will probably tell her own story in due time."

"Well, father," he spoke aloud, "please give us more of your own experience now, for I am sure we are all anxious to hear it."

As nothing else was suggested, I began: "Another important event in shaping my destiny occurred in the autumn of 1852. During the early part of September, through what I now consider to have been purely providential leadings, I went from Ticonderoga, with Joseph Cook, to Keeseville, in the northern part of the State, to attend an academy, allusion to which has already been made. We arranged to board and room together. He was not then a member of any Church, but was strictly moral and even religious, and well versed in the knowledge of the Bible. In our first Sabbath experience in the place he said to me "Will you go with me to the Presbyterian Church this morning?' I

13

hesitated a moment and then replied, "Yes, if you will go to the Roman Catholic Church with me this afternoon." 'Certainly,' he unhesitatingly answered, showing no prejudice against it. I was not a little perplexed at my dilemma, for I had a holy—rather an unholy—dread of going into a Protestant church, looking upon it as the sure way to perdition. My early teaching on the subject came up forcibly to my mind. But hoping that the harm I might incur would be more than counterbalanced by the good he might receive by going with me—for I greatly desired to convert him to my faith—I finally ratified my engagement and prepared to go with him.

"At the ringing of the bell from the old stone tower by the bridge we started. But if the air along the street had been filled with voices whispering or crying, 'Don't go! don't go!' I could not have been more influenced. It seemed as if my mother was looking at me, and pleading to stay my steps. When I had entered the vestibule of the church I shuddered, and would have turned back had it not been that, like Orpheus, who ventured to descend into Hades to deliver his wife, Eurydice, I had hopes of saving my friend. But soon the old gray-haired sexton approached us, with such a sweet smile and words so kind that I began to feel better, and he led us to a comfortable seat

That smile still lingers about my heart. Kindness is a powerful educator.

"This was an occasion never to be forgotten. The pastor's name was John Mattocks, now of St. Paul, Minnesota. The pure simplicity of the place and of the worship made a lasting impression upon my mind. All the praying, preaching, and singing were in a language I perfectly understood, and over all and through all there was a fervent, loving spirit which quite captivated me. It seemed as if the nobler sentiments and powers of my heart and mind were drawn out and exercised as I had never known them to be. I felt a deeper love to God and his creatures. My religious nature was fed and refreshed. I regarded the event as it seems to me a traveller must regard an oasis in the desert, where he slakes his thirst from pure, bubbling springs, and rests his weary frame under a lofty palm which supplies him both food and shelter. And yet withal I was perplexed. How could these feelings be reliable when such meetings had been represented to me by all my teachers as 'only evil continually?' Were my emotions the legitimate result of what I saw and heard, or was I deceived? Of one thing I felt quite sure, that these meetings had been misrepresented, whether wilfully or ignorantly I could not tell.

I was certainly none the worse for having been
there.   It could not be a sin, much less a
sacrilege or a crime, as Rev. Dr. Challoner says,
to attend such meetings.   Then I had been mis-
taught upon this subject.   Might not the same
thing be true of other subjects?   One thought
seemed to awaken another, and I experienced
the truth which I had somewhere read;—

> "'Lulled in the countless chambers of the brain,
>   Our thoughts are linked by many a hidden chain;
>   Awake but one, and lo! what myriads rise—
>   Each stamps its image as the other flies.'

Whither this mysterious train of thought would
lead me I could not have guessed."

"Did you again go to the Roman Catholic
church?" inquired Luella.

"Certainly.   We went, as we had engaged to
do in the morning.   But I was somewhat
ashamed, even then, of the contrast between the
two meetings.   Here our eyes were dazzled with
the gaudy paraphernalia of the place; with the
imposing equipage of the priest, as Dryden says,

> "'Clad in a gown that glows with Tyrian rays,'

and with the pompous ceremony.   Our ears were
filled with sounds pleasant enough to amuse,
quite operatic, perhaps, but we heard scarcely a
word that one in a hundred present could under-

stand. When I tried to apologize for this to my friend, he quoted a brief criticism of the Apostle Paul on the subject of speaking in the churches in an 'unknown tongue,' which fell like a scathing rebuke upon me, and I had nothing more to say.* But I had often vowed to be true to the Church, though I might be too weak to defend her from her enemies, and so I continued attending her services for several months, though with decreasing interest. I frequently attended a Protestant church, and with increasing benefit. It was during these days that I went with my chum to a Sunday-school, with which I was so pleased, that, as the boys sometimes say, 'I fell in love with it.'"

"And did you at once begin courting, as is generally the case?" asked Johnnie, with a roguish twinkle in his eyes.

"I am not ashamed to confess that I did, and it was not long before we wedded, nor have we ever sought to be divorced. I began to pay my visits as often as I could, though not regularly, either as a scholar or otherwise. I was still a little shy of the influence of those simple Bible lessons, for I was not yet the owner of a Bible, and, of course, I was not a Bible reader."

"What! nineteen years old, and had never read a Bible!" exclaimed Luella.

* 1 Cor., xiv.

"It is even so. I could not then have told you whether the book of Matthew was in the Old Testament or the New."

"Pray, give us the reasons why you did not read the Bible before this time."

Looking at my watch, I answered, "It is now too late, and I must reserve this question for our next interview."

XII.

The Bible — Various Versions — Luther — Jesuit
College, Montreal — Paul and Peter — Burnings
— Mike and the Priest — My First Bible.

Thy word is a lamp unto my feet and a light unto my path.—David.

WHEN we next came together, Luella
renewed her question about the Bible.
She further remarked that she could
not see why Roman Catholics did not
love and read the Bible like Protestants.
For her part, she felt all the time like singing—

> "How precious is the Book divine,
>   By inspiration given;
> Bright as a lamp its doctrines shine,
>   To guide our souls to heaven."

"You might go even further, Miss Luella,"
said Professor W., "for, truly, the Bible is the
inestimable gift of God to man, the only true
rule of our faith and practice. It is the great
lighthouse of the world."

"It is, indeed, the square," I added, "by which
we are to measure and lay out our religious
work. It is also the plumb-line seen by the

Prophet Amos in the midst of the people. Isaiah says, 'judgment also will I lay to the line, and righteousness to the plummet,' meaning, of course, the law of God, as revealed in his word. He who is unwilling to abide by this test must be false."

"As you intimate, these positions seem almost axiomatic," remarked the Professor. "It is, therefore, quite unaccountable, and very significant withal, that the Romish authorities so unanimously and decidedly oppose the Bible. It would greatly please me to hear their reasons—if they really have any—for so doing."

" The first reason I ever heard from them," I replied, "is, that the Bible is essentially a Protestant book. Hence I never heard a priest mention the word Bible without contempt. Whenever they desire to speak of their own Bibles they use the term Holy Scriptures, or Canonical Writings. In the Catechism in which I was taught there is not a word said about the Scriptures, for or against. Everything seems to be referred to the authority of the Church."

" There is not much exaggeration, then," said the Professor, " in what a friend of mine wrote me from Italy a few days ago. One paragraph of his letter was as follows: 'Even a Romish priest said to me, These gentlemen' (meaning the Pope and his council) 'have certainly simplified matters greatly They have reduced the creed to a single article—'I believe in the Pope; the Bible to a single verse—'Thou art Peter;' worship to a single observance—'Thou shalt worship the Blessed Virgin;' and duty to a single rule—'In every difficulty, consult the Sacred Congregation at Rome and obey it exactly.' "

"This is quite true, and differs from my earlier training mainly in this, that with me the Bible was wholly ignored. My mother used to spend hours in telling us that Luther, a learned but depraved monk, intending to invent a new religion suited to his lusts, wrote a book, caused it to be hidden under a tombstone in a cemetery, and then reported that, in a vision of the night, angels had revealed to him where lay the true Book of God. Accordingly search was made, the book was found, and hence our Bible and the Protestant religion. She further told us that this same Luther was tormented with the fires of hell even before his death, so that his friends were compelled to immerse him in a tub of cold water, which, however, would in a few minutes boil around his burning frame, necessitating frequent changes of the bath. So much, then, about my mother's teachings in regard to what she supposed to be the true origin of Protestantism."

"Running in a parallel line with this, and sufficiently similar to it to show their common origin, came the teaching of the priests, that the Protestant Bible is a falsified copy of the word of God. Now, here are two Bibles—King James' translation, as it is called, held as authority among Protestants, and the Douay version, held as authority in the Romish Church— and I assert, that after long and careful study and comparing of both, I find them so much alike, that, bating the notes in the Douay, and the Apocrypha, which neither the Jews nor the early Christians considered a part of the sacred Canon, it requires considerable and close scrutiny to find the difference. Protestants believe their copy to be a little the more perfect—and for good reasons, for it is translated directly from the original tongues; while the Douay is a translation from the Latin Vulgate, which was itself translated from the original Hebrew and Greek by Jerome, and subsequently revised by order of the Council of Trent. I have also two translations in French —one by Genoude, and a New Testament by Le Maistre de Sacy—both Catholic editions, and yet so few and merely verbal are the differences between the Protestant and Catholic versions in my possession, that I have but little preference for one or the other. I will venture to say, that if either one is sent out into the world without note or comment, it will become a lamp for the feet of the nations, and a light for their path."

"But how is it," inquired Monsieur Grenier, "that priests are constantly urging that the Bible is a dangerous book? Though several years a student in the College of the Jesuits in Montreal, I never saw a Bible of any kind there. The scarcity of Bibles among the Roman Catholics of Canada is proverbial."

"I remember well," I added, "that when an oath was to be administered by an officer of the law in our house once—and we were living in the village of Henryville—it took a long time to find a Bible for this purpose. And when at last it was brought in—and I think it was a Protestant copy—such a dread of it fell on us all, that I hid away in a corner behind my mother, just peeping out slyly to see what was going on and remained there trembling until the dreaded volume was removed from the house. But the priests say that it is dangerous because 'hard to be understood,' as Peter wrote in regard to some things in the epistles of Paul. However, Peter clearly shows that it is the unlearned and unstable—though possibly learned in worldly philosophy—who 'wrest these passages, as they do the other Scriptures, to their own destruction.'

The passsage does not disprove the fact of the general simplicity of the Scriptures, which Isaiah asserts are so easily understood that 'the wayfaring man, though a fool, shall not err therein,' and which Paul says to Timothy 'are able to make wise unto salvation.' "

"But the priests hold, I believe, that Peter condemns the right of private judgment in interpreting the Scriptures," he continued.

"Let us examine the passage in question." I then read from the Douay Bible as follows: "And this voice we heard brought from heaven, when we were with him in the holy mount. And we have the more firm prophetical word: whereunto you do well to attend, as to a light that shineth in a dark place, until the day dawn, and the dry-star arise in your hearts: understanding this first, that no prophecy of Scripture is made by private interpretation. For prophecy came not by the will of man at any time: but the holy men of God spoke, inspired by the Holy Ghost." I then explained as follows :—

"The plain meaning of the apostle is this: that while in the Mount of Transfiguration he heard the voice of the Father testifying to the Son's true Messiahship; and now the writings of the prophets concerning Christ are more firmly established or confirmed, showing that they wrote or spoke as they were inspired by

the Holy Ghost, and not from their own individual or private interpretation or invention, as the original word evidently signifies.
Hence the 'private interpretation' refers to the
giving or uttering of prophecy, and not to its
reception or reading by ourselves. In any event,
Roman Catholic priests and people 'will do well
to attend to these prophetic words,' as they
are exhorted to do by the inspired Peter, 'As to
a light that shineth in a dark place, until the
day dawn, and the day-star arise in their hearts.'
When I add to Peter's exhortation the command
of Christ to 'search the Scriptures,' and Luke's
commendation of the noble Bereans who studied
with blessed effect the word of truth, and Paul's
recognition of the glorious influence of Scripture
knowledge upon Timothy from his childhood,
and many other scriptural directions all agreeing with these, I am puzzled even now to account
for that teaching which led me in my childhood
to entertain such a superstitious fear of the Bible.
I once had a frightful dream in which I saw
Satan reading a Testament, and, awaking in
the midst of a feverish excitement, I believed
he was the only being in the universe that ought
to have free access to this strange book !

"Horrible as these views and feelings may
seem to you, they were nevertheless the legitimate result of my instruction upon this subject.

I had listened to many discourses by bishops and priests against the use of the Bible. This was the burden of teaching during the mission of 'Brother' Telmon, at Henryville, at the time I was received into the Order of the Scapular (See chapter viii.) And as actions always speak louder than words, permit me to give you a scrap of history concerning the operations of that zealous man. About the middle of October, 1842, by order of the Bishop of Montreal, Telmon, with his coadjutors, came to a neighbourhood in the town of Champlain, Clinton County, N. Y., known as Corbeau, whose inhabitants were nearly all French Canadians. The people had been pretty well supplied with Bibles and Testaments by means of colporteurs; hence the alleged necessity of the mission. After the meetings had progressed some days, and the priests had reached a high degree of power over the public conscience, an order was issued for the surrender of all the Bibles in the place. Some of the people refused to give up what they considered was to them a great treasure, but a sufficient number of the sacred volumes were brought to make a large bonfire, which was kindled on the twenty-seventh of the month, in open day, and in the presence of a large concourse of people.* In 1855 I had the pleasure

* For further particulars see Dowling's "History of Romanism," p. 612.

of visiting this neighbourhood and of preaching to the people, where I found some of the families who still retained their proscribed Bibles. But I found one old lady who delighted to speak of herself as an eye-witness and participant in the scenes of that conflagration, and who boasted of her 'zeal for God' by saying, 'I would run up to the burning pile, kick the Bibles further into the fire, and then fly back for fear they'd poison me!'" *

"Ah, it is plain," said the Professor gravely, "as to who is responsible for the fear which the great majority of Romanists have of the Bible. In my travels through Spain, Italy, South America, and some of the Atlantic islands, I learned of individuals and whole families who were imprisoned, and otherwise punished by the Church, for being found reading, or even possessing, a Bible. The same would undoubtedly occur in this country if Romanists were in the ascendency, and the priests had the requisite power, as 'Father'

---

* However, as the old woman thus kicked the partly-burned Bibles, charred pieces were borne aloft by the wind, and came back, like snowflakes, upon the ground. A French Canadian boy of twelve, named Louis Morin, led by curiosity, gathered a few of these fragments, and, reading them, was converted to God. He died a few years later in the triumphs of the Christian faith. Thus God protects His holy Word, whatever men may do.

Hecker, the editor of the *Catholic World*, does not scruple in public lectures and otherwise, to announce that they will have as soon as 1890, if not before ! "

"I hope not," I replied. "But permit me here to give you the last plea of the priests against the reading of the Bible by their people. They say that it is unnecessary, because they teach all that the people need to know in order to their salvation."

"But what would you think of me as the teacher of your children," added the Professor, "if I should tell them, 'You have no need of text-books to study ; all that is necessary is to listen to me ?'"

"I would have you dismissed at once if I could," I replied.

"And yet there would be more ground to justify me in pursuing this course than for the religious teacher in that, for there is scarcely any occasion for controversy in the realm of the common sciences, and even if a scientific error were inculcated it might be easily corrected ; but this is not true of religious teaching. I have always admired the sound philosophy as well as keen wit of the Irishman, whose successful controversy with his priest on this subject runs as follows : 'But,' said the priest, 'the Bible is for the priests, and not for the likes

o'you.' 'O, but, sir!' he answered, 'I was reading in my Bible, You shall read it to your
chil'ren.' 'But, Michael,' says the priest, 'you
can't understand the Bible. It is not for you
to understand it, my man.' 'Ah, very well, yer
riverence, if I can't understand it, it'll do me no
harm, and what I can understand does me a heap
o' good.' 'Very well, Mike, you must go to the
Church and the priests will teach you. The
Church will give you the milk of the word.'
'And where, indade, does the Church get it from
but out of the Bible? Ah, your riverence, I'd
rayther keap the cow meself.'"

After the subsidence of merriment which
followed the Professor's well-told story, I remarked :—

"Wherefore, then, this united and persistent
cry of the priests against the Bible in the family
and in the schools? Why do they not keep
Bibles for sale, as they do other books in
abundance? Why do they not suggest the use
of their own Bibles in the public schools if they
really object to ours, for no well-informed or
unprejudiced Protestant would object to their
introduction?"

"Ah, sir," replied the Professor, "I am convinced, as never before, that this is a crusade
against the system of our common schools itself,
and that it is the old cry of the slave-master

14

against the education of the slave. It is even like the instinct of the beast of prey which courts the darkness in which to commit its depredations. There are men who love darkness more than light because their deeds are evil. It is even doubtful whether the Pope can much longer remain in Rome amid the kindling light of the Bible. The one or the other will probably have to leave. But I think they might as well ask us to exclude sunlight and fresh air as the Bible from our schools. I admit, however, that the Bible is a dangerous book! It is dangerous to false doctrines and their teachers; dangerous to superstition, bigotry, and to civil and religious despotism; because it inspires freedom of thought and of investigation, and a sincere respect for conscience and the rights of man, and thus becomes the palladium of our liberties."

"I am sure," I added, "that it is not only an alarm-bell to awaken the careless, but also a lever to raise them up, and nerve-force to set them in motion. It supplies the chief *stimulus* and motive in every department of thought and action. 'We account the Scriptures of God,' wrote Sir Isaac Newton, 'to be the most sublime philosophy.' And yet how true is the remark of an American divine; 'The truths of the Bible are like gold in the soil. Whole generations walk over it, and know not what treasures are hidden beneath. So centuries of men pass over the Scriptures, and know not what riches lie under the feet of their interpretations. Sometimes, when they discover them, they call them new truths. One might as well call gold newly dug new gold.'"

"It was just in this light, I am sure," said Monsieur Grenier, "that the Roman Catholic Church regarded the utterances of the Reformers. They were only old, precious, but forgotten truths, long hidden in the rubbish of superstition. So I think that the Protestantism of to-day is only the re-assertion of old, apostolical truths against the innovations and errors of mediæval times, as the study of the Bible clearly shows. Here is an illustration of my meaning: A neglected urchin, with dirty hands and face, and hair uncombed, came into our school-room one day. He was taken to the wash-room and compelled to make a thorough toilet. When a mirror was placed before him he started back in surprise, and exclaimed, 'Why, I've forgotten who this is!' So, when the Reformers had done their work upon the inner life and outward appearance of the Church, the Romish heirarchy cried out, 'We don't know her!' But," abruptly turning to me, he continued, "Do tell us how you ever came to study the Bible, notwithstanding the teachings of your parents and the priests."

"These were some of my reasons. I had reached an age when I began to feel ashamed of my ignorance of what then seemed to me to be the Book of books, and the end of all controversy. It did not satisfy me to tell a man, 'I believe so and so, because the priests tell me so.' I wanted to be able to say, 'Thus saith the Lord, the great Teacher.' I felt this the more keenly, perhaps, because in all my debates with Joseph Cook, he invariably overpowered me by his thorough knowledge of the Bible. One day while bleeding from the thrust of his two-edged sword, I thus soliloquized: 'Young man, I will fight you with your own weapons!' I further reasoned in this way: 'If the doctrines of my Church are taught here'—and I did not then doubt that they were—'the more I study them, the better prepared I shall be to defend them, and to make terrible sorties on the lines of the enemy.' Impelled by such convictions I made the purchase of this little Bible, upon the blank page of which you can read this inscription: 'Keeseville, N.Y., November 13, 1852.' This book, as you can see by examination, was thoroughly studied, and it was productive of influences which I hope, on some future occasion, to be able to explain."

XIII.

"Blind Peter"—Alarmed—Bible Reading—Celi
bacy—Prophets, Apostles, etc., Married Men—
Apocalypse—My Mother in Tears—Preaching to
the Trees.

*To the law and to the testimony: if they speak not according to this
word, it is because there is no light in them.—Isaiah.*

BOTH the Professor and Monsieur Grenier
were absent from our meeting this time,
as were also Johnnie and Mary, who
had gone to visit their grandfather
in the country. But their place was
at least partially filled by a popular individual
known as "Blind Peter," who, in consequence of
his total blindness and sincere piety, is a great
favourite in the family. As his parents and
Nora's happened to be from the same parish in
Ireland, and were fast friends, who often spoke
to their children of each other, they seemed even
on their first meeting to be old acquaintances.
Peter lost no time in further influencing Nora
favourably toward himself by presenting her a
beautiful little book which bears his name and

recounts, in a simple, yet forcible style, the
eventful story of his life.   Though never a very
firm Roman Catholic even in his Emerald Isle,
and still less so after his immigration here, he
yet, like thousands of others, remained a nominal member of that Church until about twenty-
eight years of age, when he was converted and
became a sincere Protestant Christian. The sale
of his book is now his chief means of support,
and our children delight to lead him around
among the people, who generously patronize
him.   Having been here two or three days, and
hearing much said about our Sunday afternoon
interviews, he became deeply interested, and
was pleased to become a participant in our discussions.   He was a true namesake of the great
apostle, at least in his readiness to talk; and as
soon as he had been led to a chair, and all were
quietly seated, he said:—

"I'm right sorry that I have not heard your
conversations from the first.   But I hope to get
the substance of them, at any rate, in a book
some time.   And now I shall rejoice to hear you
speak, as you intimated yesterday that you
expected to do, on the influence of Bible reading
on your mind."

"I ought, perhaps, to tell you now," I replied,
"that my only desire when I began to read the
Scriptures was to fortify myself in Romanism.

The New Testament first received my attention. There was much that I did not understand, and this caused me to think that, perhaps, the priests were right in attributing obscurity to the sacred Book. But I found myself almost involuntarily reasoning on this wise: 'If I were to read a treatise on mathematics, or philosophy, or even history, how little would I understand from the first perusal. But by mastering the elementary principles and simpler rules, and gradually advancing, I might gain a tolerable knowledge of these subjects. So will I do with the Bible.' I knew it contained mysteries, but I hoped to learn what was knowable and practical. I soon found it to be a wonderful key to unlock the secrets of God's will, and of my inner life. I then saw what Paul meant by saying: 'The word of God is quick and powerful, and sharper then any two-edged sword, piercing even to the dividing asunder of soul and spirit; and of the joints and marrow, and is a discerner of the thoughts and intents of the heart.'"

"But was this 'sword of the Spirit' turned for or against Romanism?" asked Peter.

"At first it seemed to cut in every direction; for while there were passages that appeared to favour the Romish Church, I soon became greatly alarmed, not so much at the teaching of a single verse, but at the drift of entire paragraphs

against it.   For instance, every Roman Catholic
knows what prominence the priests give to
'traditions' in their general teachings.   But I
found both Matthew and Mark, also Paul to the
Colossians, and to Titus, agreeing in saying, that
'in vain they do worship God, teaching for
doctrines the commandments of men.   Thus
have ye made the commandments of God of
none effect by your tradition.' This was a cutting
blow of the Spirit's sword which I could not
parry."

"But my alarm greatly increased on reading
the following passage in one of Paul's letters to
Timothy: 'Now the Spirit speaketh expressly
that in the latter times some shall depart from
the faith, giving heed to seducing spirits and
doctrines of devils; speaking lies in hypocrisy,
having their conscience seared with a hot iron;
forbidding to marry, and commanding to abstain
from meats,' etc. 'Is it possible,' I queried,
'that even the Christian Church, or any branch
of it, can thus depart from the faith, contrary to
the teaching of the priests, who assert that the
Roman Catholic Church, at least, can never go
astray ? And, then, this departure is so great,
that instead of having recourse to the blessed
Holy Spirit, like the disobedient King Saul, they
'give heed to seducing spirits,' etc., that is, to
alleged apparitions of departed saints, and

especially of the Virgin Mary. Furthermore, those who have thus departed from the 'faith which was once delivered unto the saints' may be known by two leading characteristics, namely, they 'forbid to marry,' and 'command to abstain from meats.' These conclusions were stinging to my pride and alarming to my conscience. I found in the Douay Bible, that, by means of a note, an effort is made to apply this passage exclusively to certain small and almost unknown sects of ancient heretics, most of whom existed in the apostles' day, and held to the above errors. But it must be remembered that this falling away was to be 'in the latter times'—times remote from the days of the writer. And even if the passage applies to the sects mentioned in the note, which is not at all likely, it applies with equal force to all those who teach the same pernicious errors.

"My fears that this description was directly applicable to the Roman Catholic Church were greatly confirmed when I found in the same epistles of Paul the very sentences which identify the priests with this departure from the faith. I refer to the passages which relate to their marriage, where it is said that even 'the bishop should be the husband of one wife, the father of children, one that ruleth well his own house, having his children in subjection with all gravity.' Having read thus far, I endeavoured to believe that the bishop's 'wife' here meant the Church, which is sometimes called the spouse of Christ, and that his 'children' were the members of the Church. But further reading dissipated my fair conjecture, and left me in the midst of perplexity and alarm. 'For,' I read, 'if a man know not how to rule his own house, how shall he take care of the Church of God?' I clearly saw that 'his own house' and 'the Church of God' were two distinct realms, which ought to resemble each other, it is true; so closely, in fact, that the well-regulated family should be the perfect type of the Church, and this of heaven. Then my mind went back to the class of men whom God had generally chosen to rule his people. So far as I could learn, they were almost invariably married men. Such was the case with the patriarchs, the prophets, and the priests of Old Testament times. The apostles of our Lord were married men, as the above passage plainly intimates. We are not left, however, to mere intimations. We know that Peter, who is taken as the pattern and supposed first pope of the Roman Catholic Church, was a married man, whose wife's mother Jesus cured of a fever."

"Roman Catholic priests teach that Peter and

the other apostles forsook their wives and families to follow Christ," said Peter.

" But history denies any such assertion. The apostles undoubtedly left their families temporarily—never otherwise—when they went out upon their extensive missionary tours, as Christ intimates in his conversation with Peter on this subject. They were all undoubtedly willing to leave their families forever if necessary. But Paul, who is the only bachelor apostle we know of —unless Barnabas be another—clearly shows that it was his right, as an apostle, to be married if he chose ; that marriage is honourable in all classes ; and that it was a voluntary surrender of his privilege which kept him single. He also declares that his condition was an exception to apostolic usage. Hear what he says : ' Have we not power ' (referring to himself and Barnabas) ' to lead about a sister, a wife, as other apostles, and as the brethren of the Lord, and Cephas ? ' Rev. Dr. Challoner charges Protestants with having wilfully perverted that text. He says the word wife should be translated woman—that is, a Christian woman, a sister in Christ. Now, I acknowledge that the original word signifies woman. It is a word, however, which the Greek classic authors, whom Paul often quotes, use for wife. And if it does not mean wife here, what purpose could the word serve in the passage after the word sister has been introduced? It would only be a ridiculous tautology. Then Dr. Challoner would certainly not insist upon his rendering if he carefully reflected upon the liability of such conduct to be misconstrued — conduct that would have produced endless scandal even among the holy apostles—which he would make out Paul was trying to vindicate, namely, that of leading about a woman not his wife!"

"Ah!" exclaimed Peter, "these priests are such paragons of virtue, so far removed from the least suspicion of impure thoughts even, that they could not conceive of any impropriety, not to say scandal, in unmarried people going about in this style! But to drop this irony, don't you see how they endeavour by this interpretation both to hide the truth of the apostle's meaning, and to cover up their own conduct with the nuns?"

"Do you really believe, Peter," asked Nora excitedly, "that there is ever any improper intimacy between the priests and the 'sisters?' I have often had my suspicions, as I know many Roman Catholics have, but I have never dared express them fully."

"How can it be otherwise?" Peter replied.

" You must judge of human nature there as you do elsewhere.

" Now," I remarked, " I want to say to you that those Scriptures which bear upon the social and domestic life of the early ministers of Christ not only made me feel that the Romish Church had widely departed from the faith, but led me to fear that corruption was festering at its very fountain-head—even among its teachers. And 'like priest like people,' was a motto I often thought of. These things made me restless and unhappy. However, my fear did not culminate in a panic until I reached the seventeenth and eighteenth chapters of Revelation. I cannot now describe to you the convictions that came rushing upon me as I read those passages. From indications that lie on the very face of them, and pervade them throughout, came the unavoidable conclusion that the great city spoken of is Rome ; that the woman decked with royal purple and scarlet, with the golden chalice in her hand, who was to exert such universal power over the kingdoms of the earth, and who made merchandise of the souls of men, is no other than the Roman Catholic Church. I read the passages carefully, and trembled. I re-read them and then wept. I cannot portray the sadness and terror of that moment. Up to this time I had entertained

hopes that something might yet be able to dissipate my apprehension with regard to fatal
errors in the Church. I still continued to attend
her services, determined to cling to her to the
last; but my study of these chapters seemed to
have quite severed the knot which bound me to
her, though there still lingered a hope that I
might be mistaken.

"But from this time there sprang up in my
heart a peculiar attachment to the little Bible
which was making such disclosures to me. I felt
like saying, 'If I am wrong, let me know it.'
At this time I carried my Bible everywhere
with me, and spent all my leisure moments in
reading it. Some Sabbaths I read nearly all
day long, scarcely taking time to eat my
meals. In this inquiring and undecided state I
continued during the fall and winter of 1852-
53. The following spring I visited my friends
at Ticonderoga, and, in my sanguine and in-
genuous manner, I made frequent mention of
the things which had recently so fully possessed
my thoughts. Too great frankness in speaking my
mind is, probably, one of my faults. My mother,
especially, was thrown into a state of excitement
and alarm over me. One day I was reading
my Bible to myself, alone with my mother,
in her room. She was busy sewing; but I
saw that a great care was upon her. At length

she raised her eyes from her work, and, with a pathos I can never forget, she said, ' *O Louis! sers cette Bible; elle va te ruiner!* 'O, Louis! put away that Bible; it will ruin you!' Then she began to exhort me and to plead, until the big tears ran down her face in streams. This was one of the most fearful conflicts of my life. I loved my mother as ardently as a child can love. I also loved my Bible. I knew not what to do. Filial affection seemed likely to overpower moral obligation. There were moments when it appeared as if she might be right, and I wrong. I assured her, however, that I was actuated by the purest of motives.

"After a while I slipped the Bible into my pocket, left the house and repaired to a beautiful wood-crowned hill which overlooks a portion of Lake George, where, alone with my God, I studied the inspired word. By-and-by, impelled by an influence which I could not then interpret, I was led to select a verse, generally from Proverbs or the Epistle of James, which were at that time favourite books, the one for its diversified wisdom, the other for its practical piety, and from this text I would preach to the woods. And, truly, I never preached to more attentive audiences! The tall, well-proportioned, living trees I called saints; the distorted and decayed trees I called sinners; and thus I endeavoured to preach the Gospel both to good and bad. These were golden opportunities to my own heart and mind. Though days of conflict, they were also days of conquest."

Here ended our discussion, which was followed by an earnest prayer by Peter, who besought the Lord for light to shine especially upon those who are forsaking error and seeking the truth as revealed in the Gospel of Jesus.

XIV.

Prove all things ; hold fast that which is good.—Paul.

THE day of our gathering, filled with co-incidents which revealed the working of God's own hand among us, was peculiarly interesting. At our morning services quite a number of persons, including several Sunday-school scholars, came forward to unite with the Church on their personal profession of faith in our Lord Jesus Christ. Not least in the joy of our hearts came also Professor W. and Nora! After the administration of baptism to those who had not been thus consecrated to God in their infancy, the whole Church, in her augmented and joyful strength, joined in partaking of the Holy Communion, as was our custom to do on the first Sabbath of each month. The sermon of the oc-

15

casion was preached by the Rev. Damas Breaux, also a convert from Romanism. It was a memorable hour, making us feel as if we had fallen upon apostolic days.

When the time of our afternoon *séance* arrived—and all who had ever been with us were present—Monsieur Grenier gladly informed us that in the morning he had consummated his alliance with a branch of the Protestant Church, though not the same to which we here belonged. But he felt, as had been maintained throughout our discussions, that Protestantism is a unit on the fundamental teachings of Revelation. This information was received with great joy by us all, and it prepared the way for the Professor to remark, that two things developed in our talks here had led him to resolve upon the decisive step he had taken this morning. First, the eagerness with which he saw that Romanists like Monsieur Grenier and Nora, becoming enlightened in the teachings of the Bible, seek to identify themselves in experience and practice, notwithstanding the obstacles before them, with evangelical Churches. This made him feel ashamed of his want of interest, and convinced him of the Divine reality of experimental religion. Secondly, he was made to feel, as never before, that the great and final conflict between evangelical truth and man-devised error was to be fought out on this continent and in this country. But he added with emphasis—

"The weapons of our warfare must not be carnal—for I am fully in accord with my Quaker ancestors on this subject—but mighty through God to the pulling down of strongholds. It is a spiritual conflict, and spiritual weapons must be used. It is not that we wish to spill blood, but we desire to dissipate ignorance, prejudice, hardness of heart, until all over these lands and the world there shall be but one Shepherd and one fold. I, therefore, believe that the first duty every American owes to his country and to mankind is to 'seek the kingdom of God and his righteousness;' that is, as I understand it, to harmonize his inner and outward life with the remedial scheme of the Gospel, and to this end he should identify himself with some branch of the evangelical Church. This have I done to-day—one of the brightest and best days of my life."

As he uttered these words, Nora's eyes sparkled with a joy which she seemed utterly unable to restrain, and she exclaimed :—

"Oh ! I wish I could express myself as some of the rest of you do. Yet I can sing,—

''Tis mercy all, immense and free,
For, O my God, it found out me !'

To be saved from all our sins; how great is the blessing ! And then to know that we are saved now, by the blessed and positive witness of the Holy Spirit as I feel it in my heart to-day ! This is heaven below. Don't think me beside myself, for, like St. Paul, I am only 'speaking forth words of soberness and truth.' However, there is still a bitter ingredient in my cup—not that I had to sacrifice too much to attain to th. for one moment's heavenly bliss, such as I know, more than compensates me for the loss of all things besides; but my friends, including my dear mother, are still in the gall of bitterness, and in the bond of iniquity."

Here, choking with sobs, she could proceed no further, and I requested the Professor to lead us in prayer. Complying, he thanked God for what his grace and providence had done for us; praised him for the tokens of his presence among us to melt our hearts in tenderness toward the unsaved, and closed with an earnest plea, which elicited several hearty amens, that our dear friends might soon be partakers of like precious faith with us, and that this land might ere long become as the garden of the Lord. At the close of this delightful exercise, there being a general desire that I should return to my personal narrative, I resumed :—

" After becoming convinced of many errors in

the Church, I began to read the Bible, as it seems to me it ought always to be read if great good is desired, not to establish some preconceived theory or dogma, but simply to learn the mind of the Spirit who inspired it, or the scope of truth in the mind of the sacred writer. Influenced by such an endeavour I began to search and study. The doctrine of images in the churches was one of the first that presented itself for review. I had been taught that we may honour the images of the saints as well as their relics. In her offices for the dying, the Church directs that a crucifix be often looked upon and kissed, and that an image of the Virgin Mary be placed before the eyes, that recourse may be had to her. In all the French Catechisms I have ever seen, the second commandment, namely, 'Thou shalt not make unto thee any graven image.... Thou shalt not bow down thyself to them nor serve them,' etc., is entirely omitted."

"But that must leave only nine commandments," quickly remarked Johnnie.

"The Church," I added, "has ingeniously divided the tenth commandment into two parts, thus preserving the original number, but making two which are alike in spirit."

"Such mutilation and rending of holy writ," exclaimed Aunt Melie, "is dreadful to think of, and must bring upon the Church which dares attempt it the swift judgments of God!"

"Think of my own indignation toward a Church that could purposely be guilty of such gross perversion of truth, when I found the direct command of God against this practice. This mandate is still further explained and enforced by several sacred writers both in the Old and New Testaments. It is not enough that most Romish authors, including Dr. Challoner, who covers nearly seven pages of his book in defence of this devotion, should say that they do not worship the image; this is only pettifogging."

"Even admitting, for the sake of the argument," said the Professor, "that this plea be true, it is saying no more than heathens generally claim for themselves. Most of them assert that they do not worship the manikin, but the Diety it represents. So the Ephesians whom Paul encountered on this question of idolatry were worshippers of the great goddess Diana, whose image was supposed to have fallen down from Jupiter. It was the goddess, not the image, which was the object of their homage. The same was true of the Athenians, whose altar or shrine was inscribed 'To the Unknown God.'"

"Your remarks are pertinent, Professor, or

rather, brother in Christ, as I ought to call you now. I cannot see how the Romish Church can be exonerated from the charge of idolatry. Dr. Challoner endeavours to wriggle out of this dilemma by saying that 'those whom the Roman Catholics honour with an inferior veneration for God's sake,' those before whose images they offer prayers, 'are, indeed, the ministers and servants of the one true God, while the inferior deities of the heathens were wicked wretches, such as Mars, Bacchus, Hercules, etc.'"

"Now I aver," again said the Professor, "that the only logical deduction that can be drawn from the doctor's own premise is, that Romanism and heathenism are two great idolatries, and that they differ only in degree; Romanism being more elevated and refined in proportion as its inferior deities are more pure than those of heathenism. This is not the first time this criticism has occurred to me, and though it may seem severe, I am sure it cannot be successfully obviated."

"My study of the images of the saints and their relation to pure worship soon led me to its cognate branch, namely, the prayers to the Virgin Mary, and to the multitude of the saints. The Romish Church puts in the plea here that she does not worship these saints, but simply requests their prayers, as we do each other's prayers on earth. To this point I directed my examination. In the litanies to the Virgin, as found in the prayer-book, entitled 'Way to Heaven,'* pages 60 and 574, she is called 'Seat of Wisdom, Cause of our Joy, Ark of the Covenant, Gate of Heaven, Morning Star, Refuge of Sinners, Seat of the Most Holy Trinity, Image of the Wisdom of God, Dispenser of Graces, Model of all Perfection, Source of Divine Love,' etc. In the same book, page 388, the third of six fundamental rules laid down for the guidance of the Arch-confraternity of the Holy and Immaculate Heart of Mary, reads as follows: 'No intercession is so effectual as that of the blessed mother of God; let us, therefore, seek it.' On page 77 we find this prayer: 'Oh! my Lady, holy Mary, to thy blessed keeping, and to the bosom of thy tender compassion, I commend my soul and body this day, every day, and at the hour of my departure; all my hopes, my consolation, my anxieties and miseries, my life and the end of my life, I commit to thy keeping,' etc. On page 389 is this: 'Come, O my soul, prostrate thyself at the feet of Mary thy Mother, and depart not till she hath blessed thee.' On the next page a family is offered to Mary in these terms: 'Most

* Approved by † John, Archbishop of New York.

blessed Virgin, our immaculate Queen and Mother, refuge and consolation of the distressed, prostrate before thy throne, with all my family, I choose thee as my patroness, my mother, and my advocate with God. I consecrate myself forever, with all that belongs to me, to thy service.' Many similar passages might be quoted from the same book, to show that, in the matter of consecrating ourselves and families to her, Mary is put in the place of God the Father. She is also represented as God, sitting on a throne. In the titles which are given her, and the intercession attributed to her, she is put in the place of Christ the Son. The artists of the Church also represent the woman instead of her seed, as bruising the serpent's head. On page 415, in an article entitled 'Divine Praises,' arranged for choral responses, the Virgin occupies the place of the Holy Ghost. The article runs as follows, and one year's indulgence is granted for every recital :—

" 'Blessed be God.'

"' Blessed be his holy name.'

" ' Blessed be Jesus Christ, true God and true man.'

" ' Blessed be the name of Jesus.'

" ' Blessed be Jesus in the most holy Sacrament of the altar.'

"'Blessed be the great Mother of God, the most holy Mary.'

"'Blessed be the name of Mary, Virgin and Mother.'

"'Blessed be God in his angels and in his saints.'"

"This is not only idolatry," cried Aunt Melie, "but the grossest blasphemy. It falls not short of what I deem to be the sin against the Holy Ghost. It makes me tremble with horror to hear it!"

"We need no more proof," added Monsieur Grenier, " to fix upon Romanists the charge of worshipping the Virgin Mary."

"And yet," I continued, "lest some one should say that this representation is not complete, let me turn to page 622 of the book just quoted for the final proof upon this subject. Here is a prayer with this significant heading: 'To the Worshippers of the Most Blessed Virgin, Mother of God.' At the close of the prayer, in which there is language more trustful and adoring than in anything yet quoted, we find these sentences in italics: 'So says the sweet St. Bernard. Worship, then, the Mother of God in thy life, and thou shalt feel that thou has worshipped one who is truly a Mother, in death and in all eternity. For to be worshipped and regarded as a Mother is assuredly her delight. For that she might be the Mother and Mediatress of sinners it was that she became the Mother of God.'

"Imagine now, if you can, what were my feelings, after having been taught such doctrines as these, to find directly opposite teachings in the word of God. When the Magi found the Nazarene family in the Bethlehem manger, they worshipped the child only. So did the shepherds. When the child was lost at Jerusalem at the close of the passover feast, Mary knew no more where he was than any other mother would have known of her child. After he entered his public ministry, all that Jesus ever said about his mother, though couched in dutiful and respectful language, was evidently intended to check every tendency toward worshipping her. For instance, when a certain woman of the company that followed him lifted up her voice and said unto Him: 'Blessed is the womb that bare thee, and the paps which thou hast sucked'—that is, blessed is thy mother—he said, 'Yea, rather blessed are they that hear the word of God, and keep it.' Christ is to be known, not after the flesh, but by faith and love. This is made very clear in the passage where he said, 'Who is my mother? and who are my brethren? And he stretched forth his hand toward his disciples, and said: Behold my mother and my brethren. For whosoever shall do the will of my Father which is in heaven, the same is my brother, and sister, and mother.'

"When the disciples besought Christ to teach them to pray, he said, 'When ye pray, say, Our Father who art in heaven,' etc., and he never taught them any other prayer. How could he make an omission so grave if Romanism be correct? Just before his departure he said to them: 'Whatsoever'—and this covered all their possible needs for the present and for all time to come—'whatsoever ye shall ask the Father in my name, he will give it you.' All recorded prayers of the apostles were addressed to the Deity. When, on the Isle of Patmos, St. John would have worshipped the angel who made revelations to him, he was forbidden: 'See thou do it not; worship God,' said his heavenly visitant. How this array of Scripture facts, taught in the Douay Bible as well as in all others, could be reconciled with the teachings of the Church, was more than I could comprehend. I found here a point-blank contradiction which no sophistry could remove or obscure."

"But Roman Catholic priests plead," remarked Nora, "that as our mothers are generally more tender toward us than our fathers, so the Virgin Mother is more readily touched with the feeling of our infirmities than is the Father."*

* See the prayer-books.

" O ! I know how strongly this manner of putting the subject appeals to our capricious and youthful sympathies. There is wonderful power in woman's tenderness, especially a mother's. I have seen vast multitudes melted into tears by the adroit and earnest priest who desired to lead the people to the shrines of the Virgin, especially in her 'Novenas,' or nine days' devotions. But to the thoughtful student of the Bible such reasoning is sophistical and silly. It pre-supposes that Mary is omnipresent and omniscient ; for she must be everywhere, in order to hear the million prayers of the scattered multitudes that simultaneously call upon her ; and she must know all things, to be able to read the thoughts of their hearts. But if she possess these attributes, she is equal with God. All this is unscriptural and false. It further presumes that one, at least, of God's creatures is more perfect in compassion, and more full of mercy, than the Creator himself, which is ludicrous as well as sacrilegious. But keep in mind, Nora, that God loves to be inquired of for all the things we need, and that he yearns over all His children with a compassion more tender and constant than ever gushed even from a loving mother's heart. He who gave mothers their tenderness must be more tender than they :—

" ' Every human tie may perish ;
Friend to friend unfaithful prove ;
Mothers cease their own to cherish ;
Heaven and earth at last remove ;
But no changes
Can attend Jehovah's love.' "

"Indeed, sir, I know it now, but I have not always realized it. It scarcely seems that I am the same person I was once. I seem to be in a new world. How quickly and beautifully my heart now interprets what was difficult before. Truly, I am a new creature: 'Old things have passed away; behold all things have become new!' But I fear that by my ecstatic outbursts I am interrupting your narrative."

" 'Variety is the spice of life,' Nora," responded Luella, "and I'm sure we all enjoy this kind of spicing. So don't borrow any trouble about it. When God's love burns in our hearts, it is often difficult to keep from speaking or singing. And yet, perhaps, we would all be glad to hear from father now if you are through."

"Through! If I had a thousand tongues I would want them all to sing my great Redeemer's praise, and even then it seems as if all eternity would be too short to tell the story of Jesus and his love. As we often sing,—

" ' More wonderful it seems
Than all the golden fancies
Of all our golden dreams.'

"But, really," she continued, turning to me,
"please excuse me for delaying you so much."

"God bless your soul, Nora!" exclaimed
Blind Peter. "As the gardens of myrrh and
sweet spices are stirred by the soft zephyrs of
heaven, so your inspired words move my heart
until it sighs more solemnly than the harp of
Judah's royal bard."

On the utterance of this poetic and religious
sentiment it seemed as if a Divine joy rested on
every one, and we almost involuntarily broke
forth in singing our grand doxology :—

"Praise God, from whom all blessings flow ;
Praise him, all creatures here below ;
Praise him above, ye heavenly host ;
Praise Father, Son, and Holy Ghost."

When the singing ceased, I said :—

"In advancing toward the Divine or truly
Christian life, I went more slowly than most of
you seem to have done. I clung to old things
with an almost dogged pertinacity, while my
great caution suffered me to accept nothing new
without the severest tests. When one doctrine
was fairly wrenched from me by the force of
truth, another would come up for examination.
Prayers before images and saints having been
disposed of, the doctrine of Purgatory presented
itself for analysis. Romish authorities give
this definition of the doctrine : 'A middle state

of souls who depart this life in God's grace. yet not without some lesser stains of guilt or punishment, which retard them from entering heaven.' Then it is claimed that 'such as depart this life before they have repented of these venial frailties and imperfections, cannot be supposed to be condemned to the eternal torments of hell, nor can they go straight to heaven in this state, because the Scripture assures us, 'There shall not enter into it anything defiled.'* Then an attempt is made at proof from Scripture, tradition, and reason. So I went to work examining the doctrine by this triple light. To my astonishment, I found that the Bible makes no such distinction as this doctrine implies between what are called mortal and venial sins. 'Sin,' says the word, 'is the transgression of the law,' and 'he who offends in one point is guilty of all;' that is, every sin is a violation of God's law, and merits the punishment which the law, as a whole, inflicts. Again, the Scriptures recognize but two general classes of men, namely, saints and sinners, wheat and tares, sheep and goats; those who are for Christ, and those who are against him. No middle class is ever as much as intimated in them.

" Then the Bible presents but one element for

* "Grounds," etc., p. 46.

the purging or purifying of sin and uncleanness —the blood of Jesus Christ. Nowhere could I find that fire, unless it be used emblematically of the Holy Spirit, can cleanse moral stains; much less can general suffering do this. Suffering may mature graces, but cannot produce them. Suffering people are not necessarily, nor even generally, the purest people. The angel said to John, ' These are they which came out of great tribulation ; ' but he does not attribute their salvation to their sufferings, as the closing words do show : 'and have washed their robes, and made them white in the blood of the Lamb.' None in that vast throng are heard praising the flames of purgatory or the indulgences of the Church, but all ascribe glory to the Lamb. Furthermore, the Bible taught me that in this life only can sins be loosed or forgiven. ' Behold, now is the accepted time ; behold, now is the day of salvation.' After death the order is, ' He that is filthy, or defiled, let him be filthy still.' These are all fundamental principles which cannot be gainsayed, and they all and severally proved to me that the doctrine of purgatory is a figment. This doctrine, like many others in Romanism, is plainly traceable to Plato, Virgil, and many other ancient heathen authors, from whom the Church borrowed it.

16

"Intimately connected with this doctrine is that of indulgences; which, as latterly interpreted by the Church, ' is not a leave to commit sin, nor a pardon for sins to come, but only a releasing of the debt of temporal punishment which may remain due on account of our sins, after the sins themselves, as to the guilt and eternal punishment, have been already remitted by contrition, confession, and absolution.' Such a doctrine, as applied to individual—not to national—transgression, I, of course, nowhere found in the Bible. And it is so vaguely expressed, even by the best writers of the Church, that but few are able to understand it. But they are made to feel that there is something wrong with them for which they can make atonement for themselves and for others, by repeating more prayers and performing more good works than are required in the Scriptures."

"This is curious," remarked Luella, "that any person can do even more than God requires, when he commands us to love and serve him with all our heart and mind and strength. I remember reading—yes, it was in our Sunday-school lesson this afternoon—that Jesus said to his disciples, ' When ye shall have done all these things which are commanded you, say, We are unprofitable servants : we have done that which was our duty to do.' "

" This very passage made me see the folly of this doctrine. However, the Church so arranges her list of indulgences, as you can see in ' Way to Heaven,' page 13, that a devoted Roman Catholic can gain a large number of plenary indulgences each year, to apply to the future advantages of himself or others. A plenary indulgence is one that remits the full punishment due to sin, and hence delivers the recipient fully and forever from the flames of purgatory. But as the Bible taught me to look to the Lamb of God alone for salvation, I saw that this doctrine was only a degenerate offspring of the vagary of purgatory. So much, then, did I get from the argument from Scripture."

" The argument from Tradition," added Monsieur Grenier, " certainly fixes this innovation to a period some centuries after the time of the apostles, who were wholly innocent, as it appears, of any such teaching. And no wonder the Church resorted to it when one considers the revenues it brings into her coffers. This of itself shows where the doctrine originated. Here is her costly merchandise of souls.* About one· dollar is the least amount usually paid for a low mass for the dead. A high

* Apoc., xviii. 12, 13.

mass is much more expensive, and varies with the ability of the payer and the dignity of the officiating clergyman. The profligate Philip IV., King of France, left money for ten thousand masses to be chanted for the repose of his soul."

"I see now," said Johnnie, "why this is called the 'religion of money.' But it is a new idea that men may buy with money a seat in heaven. That being the order, I don't see much chance for the poor; and yet nearly all the Roman Catholics that I know are poor."

"Many are made so in this way," I replied. "Poor as was my widowed mother, she paid for masses for the repose of my father's soul long after his death, and continued to pray for the same object several years later. There is scarcely a widow, however poor, that would not go to the expense of at least one mass. Some would sell their own bedding and bread for this purpose, before they would leave their friends unassisted in purgatory. Many people agree by solemn covenant that the survivors shall pay for a stipulated number of masses, and pray so many years for those who first go down to the purgatorial abode. I believe that such an agreement existed between my father and mother."

"Those priests who are at the bottom and the top of all that," exclaimed Aunt Melie, "are perfectly described by the great Teacher when he said, 'Woe unto you! for ye devour widows' houses, and for a pretence make long prayers.' I can find no language to express my indignation! They are blind guides, leading the blind into the ditch."

"But I am not quite through with my work. I must give you my argument from Reason. This taught me that if purgatory had been established by the Lord, he would have regulated its internal affairs himself; but now the priests dictate the terms upon which men may escape its tortures, and this shows whose establishment it is. Reason further taught me that, if account were made of the vast number of masses for the dead, and the endless grant of indulgences, supposing there were any truth in the doctrine, purgatory must long ago have been completely emptied of its souls, and made a void. And yet the people continue to pray and pay, and the priest continues to take the money and to say the masses! But the stamp of error, not to say of deception, was put upon the dogma when Reason presented it to me in this light: Suppose that I saw one of my fellow-men drowning or in flames, and, standing near, should cry to him, 'Pay me money and I will help you, but otherwise I will leave you to your fate,' what would you think of me?"

"Heartless! Villainously criminal you surely would be," responded Luella, with an energy almost unnatural to her.

"What, then, could be my thoughts and feelings toward a Church that legislates the vast multitude of her members into purgatorial flames, and leaves them there unless the dead have left her money by bequest, or their friends rally to their aid with an open purse?"

"And yet this is the Church," added the Professor, "that says to the world," 'I am the only true Church of God; apostolical in succession infallible in doctrine, holy in practice!'"

"If there be truth in her teaching and power in her prayers," said Luella, "why don't she try her skill first upon her living subjects, and then whether she succeeds or fails, if she thinks best to pray for the dead, do so every day without pay?"

"She does condescend," I replied, "to say masses for the dead gratuitously one day in the year—on All-Souls' Day, the second of November."

"Thanks! thanks!" cried several voices, and Aunt Melie continued by saying; "This is quite relieving. Crumbs are better than no bread at all. There is some hope of a Church that consents to pray for her needy children one day in the year without special pay!"

"Your sarcasm does not half express the feelings that were in my heart when I saw this subject in its true light. At this point of my investigation I was completely cut loose from Romanism; for every faculty of my soul rejected these abhorrent teachings, and I could not conscientiously affiliate with those who taught or believed them."

With the close of this discussion the time had come to disperse.

XV.

Danger and Rescue—Romanism and Infidelity—
Seeking the True Fold — Weeping, Reading,
Praying — Wonderful Night — To be "Born
Again"—Dream in Verse.

Marvel not that I say unto thee, Ye must be born again.— The Master.

ON meeting again to-day, where we found
our entire company except Blind Peter,
the Professor, anticipating the chaos into which I must have plunged on losing
all confidence in the Romish Church,
inquired how my mind was affected by the
change.

"Danger," I replied, "attends every change
in life, from the cradle to the grave. Even the
seasons as they succeed each other generally
occasion vast commotion in the elements and
fearful storms. This is especially true in mental and moral transitions. 'Changes and war
are against me,' exclaimed the old patriarch Job,
and even I was not exempt from similar experience. At first I yielded to a dull despair which

tended to blank infidelity! All the hope of heaven I had ever entertained had been founded upon Romanism. As the errors and follies of the system passed before me, my hope dissolved like frost-work on the window-panes in the sun-beams until all was gone! In consequence, I found myself losing all confidence in men. From childhood my best teachers, including my parents, had deceived me, whether willfully or ignorantly made but little difference. Whom now could I trust? Would strangers be more true than friends had been? Dread distrust and black misanthropy were creeping in upon me. In my haste, like one of old, I said, 'All men are liars,' and 'none really care for my soul.' Religion began to appear to me an ugly, mocking mummery; a monstrous priestcraft, dwarfing the intellects of men by repressing true education and culture, by proclaiming a false philosophy and corrupt ethics, and by making promises it never could fulfill. It was to me a filthy harpy, which soiled what it did not devour."

"This was the terrible yet natural rebound from one extreme to the other," added the Professor. "'The mind of communities,' says an American author, 'touches both extremes before it settles down at the intermediate point of truth.' History shows that the enlightenment of Roman Catholic peoples has always had infidelity for its immediate fruit. Witness France, with her Volney and Voltaire, and her 'Reign of Terror.' Most of the educated classes in all papalized countries to-day are evidently infidel at heart. And yet those who have vibrated so far from the 'central point of bliss,' as our author intimates, have often rested, at last, at the 'golden mean' where they have found what neither meaningless mummeries on the one hand, nor blind infidelity on the other, could furnish."

" Indeed, God in his great mercy did not leave me in my blindness and misery to perish. He gave me burdens only as I could bear them, and blessings only as I could appropriate and enjoy them. When I began to mutter this dirge-like song of doubt:—

> "'There is no good ; there is no God ;
> And Faith is a heartless cheat,
> Who bares the back for the Devil's rod,
> And scatters thorns for the feet,'—

I advanced to the very verge of the yawning abyss of scepticism, but was driven back by its horrifying darkness and terror ! My religious nature would somehow cling to the belief in a Supreme Being, the First Great Cause, the Father of the race. 'Then,' I reasoned, 'if there be a God, he must in some way have revealed his will to his children, as in the Bible, for instance, and there must be some organization on earth which, in the main at least, embodies and illustrates this teaching.' Thus convinced, I was led to attend the services of the different churches in the village of Keeseville, and by this means to the discovery that the various Protestant denominations are essentially one, differing only, perhaps, as the strings of a harp differ from each other, and yet all needed to give to music its grandest power and harmony.

"One Sabbath I went to the Methodist Church, and, to my surprise, I found the Baptist preacher in the pulpit, by exchange. This produced a very salutary influence upon my mind. And then the fact that these services supplied the food for which my spirit hungered was another evidence of truth in these Churches, such as abstract reasoning could not well give me.

"On Sunday evening, November 6, 1853, after attending several services, I returned to my room with more than an ordinary degree of religious thoughtfulness. I sat down to write my journal for the day. Fearing that, in case any one should ever read those lines, he might be at a loss to account for my instability as to the places where I went for public worship, I undertook to give my reasons in the following manner: ' When at home, I was brought up in the strictest observance of Romanism. A few years' experience in a Protestant land has wrought a great change in me. I am now convinced that my former faith and practice are fundamentally unscriptural, at least in their spirit and application to soul-saving; and I have come to the conclusion that, ere I follow any religious leaders, I must first ascertain whether I am led by the blind, or by those who have eyes to see. This prompts me to make careful investigation, and to wander from church to church, until I find the 'Good Shepherd's' fold. O! how I long to be freed from this fearful mist of uncertainty, and to find that rest which my soul has never known! Such wanderings as these torture me, and here and now I pray for guidance and deliverance. I know I can do nothing of myself toward coming to God, but may he help and save me. My determination is so strong that, if I find I must renounce my former faith for another, though it bring upon me censure from all my relatives, I shall pledge myself and bind my heart. This, however, is a difficult question to settle. I have a tender mother whom I love. O! how soon would she be brought with sorrow to the grave if I should wander from the teachings she has so laboriously imparted to me. Apprehensive of this, she has already mourned and wept. During my last visit to her she pleaded with me with many earnest words and scalding tears. (I weep while I record it.) How could I treat her so ill? No! I will not. So long as she lives I cannot publicly profess such a change, whatever resolves I may carry in my breast.'

"At this point in my record my tears were blinding me and failing fast upon the memorable page. I laid down my pen, not knowing what to do. My heart was overwhelmed with sadness. I was alone! Soon, moved as if by a Divine impulse, I seized my little Bible and the candle, and going to my bedside I knelt and resolved to read whatever chapter the book should open at. I then read and prayed and wept in succession for some time."

"Do you remember what passage you happened to find?" asked Johnnie, whose cheeks were bedewed with tears.

"I cannot well forget it. The evening interview of Nicodemus with Jesus especially attracted my attention. The more I read and studied it, the more interested I became. Like Nicodemus, I felt I was holding intercourse with the Master, and like him I was confounded with the spirituality and depth of his teaching. I was made to see and feel that my religion had been a mere shell—a superficial and generally defective form, without power. This was especially true with regard to my prayers, and with most of the religious services I had performed in church. For these were in Latin, so that they were necessarily repeated much as a parrot might do it. The same was true with regard to my previous views of the Lord's Supper. I had been taught that I must eat the body of my Lord, in the same manner in which ordinary bread is eaten."

"Why, father," remarked Luella, "wouldn't that be worse cannibalism than savages are guilty of ? They eat the flesh of their fellows, but we never read of their eating the flesh of their gods!"

"Of this you must judge for yourself. But I began to see the meaning of Christ's words when he said, ' Your fathers did eat manna,' as other food is eaten, ' in the wilderness and are dead.' Then, speaking of himself, he said, ' This is that bread which came down from heaven : not as your fathers did eat manna,' —that is, not in the same way of eating, with the gross organs of the body,—' not as your fathers did eat manna and are dead : he that eateth of this bread shall live forever.' This bread, then, I saw was spiritual bread, and must be partaken of spiritually and not physically. For Paul says, ' There is a natural body, and there is a spiritual body.' It is the spiritual body of Christ which we are to eat by faith.

And my conclusion was confirmed by that saying of Jesus: 'The words that I speak unto you, they are spirit and they are life.' I further discovered that 'eating his flesh and drinking his blood' was synonymous with 'believing on him,' for to both he attaches the same result. Thus, 'he that believeth on me hath everlasting life,' and 'whoso eateth my flesh and drinketh my blood hath eternal life.' The Revelator represents Christ as saying, 'Behold I stand at the door and knock: if any man hear my voice, and open the door, I will come in to him, and will sup with him, and he with me.' Paul explains this by saying, 'That Christ may dwell in your hearts by faith.' Again: 'Christ liveth in me, and the life which I now live in the flesh I live by the faith of the son of God, who loved me and gave himself for me.' I saw, too, that this saving faith is the most simple, and yet the most mighty, thing known upon earth. For Christ said to Nicodemus, 'And as Moses lifted up the serpent in the wilderness,' so that the dying Hebrews, simply looking upon it, might be healed—an historic event which Nicodemus well understood—'even so must the Son of man be lifted up, and whosoever believeth in him,' or looketh unto him, though from the uttermost parts of the earth, 'should not perish, but have eternal life.'

" But it was in regard to this subject of being ' born again,' or, ' from above,' that my super-ficiality was especially noticeable. . I had al-ways been taught that the baptism of water had made me a Christian, that is, that I was born again, or regenerated, at the time and in virtue of my baptism.   This, I saw, was giving to the term water, which is used but once in this won-derful dialogue, altogether too much prominence. I now realized that it was used as a mere symbol of the cleansing and refreshing influences of the Spirit upon the truly born again ; just as fire, in John the Baptist's prophecy, ' He shall baptize you with the Holy Ghost and with fire,' is evidently not to be interpreted literally, but as presenting the vivifying and enlightening power of the Spirit upon those whom Christ saves.   I was made to feel that this re-creation was the special work of the Holy Ghost, as mysterious as the conception of Christ had been, which no man could explain any more than Nicodemus could tell whence came, or whither went, the winds.   ' For so is every one that is born of the Spirit.'   This change, I saw, is as necessary as it is wonderful.   This is evi-dent from the abrupt manner of Christ's question to Nicodemus, as well as by the matter of it. As there can be no physical life without a physi-cal birth, so I saw that there could be no spiritual life without a spiritual birth 'That which is flesh is flesh, and that which is spirit is spirit;' each created and subsisting by agencies and laws peculiarly its own. But the crowning interest in my study of the passage was reached when I found that this radical change was to be divinely attested; that it might be as clearly known and felt as Nicodemus felt the passing breeze, the Holy Ghost bearing witness with our spirit that, though once enemies of God and children of wrath, now we are children of God, 'born by a new celestial birth,' and 'heirs of immortality.' If I would enjoy this inestimable blessing, I saw that I must not be ashamed of Christ, but must come out of darkness into the light, and look to him alone for the recreating power. Several hours of the night passed away in these solemn meditations; and I finally retired, but more to think and weep and pray than to sleep. From that time to this I have not ceased to read and study the Bible on my knees, while looking to God with the prayer of the psalmist, 'Open thou mine eyes, that I may behold wondrous things out of thy law.'

"This nightly interview with Jesus, and almost vision of divine things, gave a pleasing check to my sceptical tendencies. The Sabbath

following, I made this entry in my journal:
' Were it possible for me to give an adequate
idea of my present state of mind, volumes
might be filled. But time will not permit me
to say more than this: I will seek salvation
though a thousand worlds oppose!' This resolu-
tion greatly stimulated me, and seemed to sweep
away every barrier that obstructed my way.

"On the twenty-first of November I began to
teach school where I had taught the previous
winter, near the village of Clintonville. There,
in the personal piety and influence of one of
the citizens of the district, Mr. James Mace,
whose religion was not a mere profession, nor a
routine of duties mechanically performed, but
the golden thread that made the warp and woof
of his everyday life, I found the next great help
to rescue me from unbelief, and to guide me to
the Saviour. I am sure that a holy life is
one of God's brightest beacon lights in this
lower world, mighty to confound infidelity, and
to establish the kingdom of the Redeemer. This
man's conversation and manners at home and
abroad—for I was much in his company—not
only instructed and delighted me, but led me
to the conclusion that he was in possession of
a precious something to which I was a stranger.
O, how I longed to know the secret of his joys!

" Through his means I was invited to take a class in the Sunday-school at Clintonville. After some hesitation and study—for I felt incompetent to the task, having never belonged to such an institution even as a scholar—I consented to do so. This brought me nearer the warm heart of the Church, and made the more careful study of the Bible, by means of maps and commentaries, a necessity. Thus my mental and moral faculties were drawn out and developed side by side, and in about equal proportion. With the closing days of the year a series of extra meetings began in the Church, under the pastoral labours of the Rev. Benjamin Pomeroy. For several days, though an interested attendant upon the services, I took no active part. But I was strangely attracted to the meetings. 'No wonder,' I wrote in my journal, 'the lamb loves the grassy mead where it feeds, and the sparkling fountain where it may daily quench its thirst.' My spiritual nature was being disencumbered of superstition, and my eyes enlightened to see the path of duty. One evening, after returning from the Church, I wrote the following stanzas :—

" ' 'Tis sweet to hold converse with Him
Who holds us in His power;
'Tis sweet to yield our souls to Him
In night's serenest hour.

17

" '"Tis then His Spirit draweth nigh,
  And folds us to His breast ;
He wipes the tears from sorrow's eye,
  And gives the spirit rest.'

My heart was in a constant spirit of prayer, desiring to be led by the wisdom of God alone.   I
was not yet converted, or ' born again,' and yet
it seemed as if but one step more would bring
me to the desired goal.   One night I had a
strange dream, which quite fully explained
my condition.   The next day I tried to express
it in poetry ; and though my efforts may lack
many of the elements of polished verse, you will,
I hope, excuse the style, and treasure up its
substance while I read it from my journal."   I
then took my third volume, from which I read
as follows :—

" ' I dreamed that from this world I flew,
    Through airy tides and sky of blue ;
    That angels lent me wings of light
    To bear me onward in my flight.

" ' The more I rose above the earth,
    The more my spirit neared its birth :
    For angels told me of a love
    That only reigns supreme above.

" ' Up, up we rose through deep expanse,
    Till worlds of light around did glance,
    And all the sky began to blaze,
    Filling my soul with dread amaze.

" ' This blaze was not from scorching fire,
  Nor of the Father's kindled ire—
  But 'twas of Love's own purest glow,
  Such love as ne'er is found below.

" ' Faint grew my heart—dazzled my sight—
  My spirit trembled—gone its might—
  Yet in despair I raised a cry,
  Whose echo shook the very sky:

" ' O, God, I ne'er can see thy face,
  Unless my heart be purged by grace!
  And now to earth I fall—I fall—
  O! send thy angels as I call.

" ' With startled pace quick flew my guide,
  Who instantly stood by my side,
  And aided my return to earth,
  Where my soul must, in time, have birth.

* * * *

" ' All ye who Christian faith pretend,
  Leave all things else— to this attend:
  O! seek the kingdom, first, of heaven—
  The grace through faith in Christ now given.

" ' For if your flight too soon should come,
  You cannot reach that blessed home,
  For God will not have aught to do
  With hearts not good, nor pure, nor true.' "

With the recitation of this simple yet impressive dream, and its moral, our interview closed.

XVI.

RESTING AT LAST—NORA AND HER BROTHER—THEO-
DORE—THE ALTAR—*Coûte que Coûte*—SAVING FAITH
—"JOY UNSPEAKABLE."

But what things were gain to me, those I counted loss for Christ. Yea, doubtless, and I count all things but loss for the excellency of the knowledge of Christ my Lord.—*Paul.*

THE week had been full of trials to our faith and patience, especially Nora's. But like the oak in storms, these virtues had taken deeper root. Several at-tempts, most ingeniously planned, had been made to remove ·her from us, but in vain. Here is a specimen. One day a close carriage was driven to the gate, from which alighted a gentleman of middle age, who proved to be one of Nora's brother's, a sea-captain, whom she had not seen for many years, and scarcely re-cognized. He was greeted with great cor-diality and friendship by her, and introduced to the family. After considerable chatting on various topics, Nora, whose heart is always glowing with her new-found hope, and full of the priceless enjoyment of the pure and undefiled religion of the Bible, told her brother, in a child-like and touching manner, the story of her conversion to Jesus, and of her membership in a Protestant Church. He was evidently moved by the fervent, straightforward narrative, but affected never to have heard of it before. Then he suggested that, as he was very anxious to hear more of these interesting particulars, if she would get ready and go with him to a neighbouring city, whither his business called him, she could relate her beautiful experience more fully during the few hours of their ride; otherwise he would not be able to visit much longer, for he must soon be going. Plausible as all this appeared, Nora was not inclined to accept the invitation without probing the matter a little more deeply. Had it been the first attempt, and no threats of abduction ever been made, it undoubtedly would have succeeded. But birds are seldom caught the second time in the same snare, though its appearance be ever so much changed or disguised. Seeing that his proposition was not acceptable, he grew a little restless, and said he must go, but that he had reserved the best news for the last. He then told Nora that Providence had given him favouring breezes; that during the Franco-Prussian war he had acquired a princely fortune while navi-

gating the waters of the contending parties; that
he had just purchased a palatial residence in
New York for their father, whose declining years
should be relieved of the shame and want re-
sulting from former misfortunes, and that now
he was ready to settle a munificent annuity upon
his brothers and sisters who were willing to
spend the remainder of their lives together in
the metropolis. To corrobrate his statement, he
exhibited deeds of the property recently purchased; and his pocket-book revealed that he
was not a stranger to gold and its equivalents in
large amounts.

Nora looked on him for a few moments in
mute astonishment. Then straightening herself
up into a majestic attitude, and gazing upon him
with her deep blue eyes, which, especially when
she was greatly moved, would remind one of the
azure sky when the clouds have just been reft,
she said :—

" Brother "—and there was such a pathos in
her tone that it seemed to pierce his heart—
"you compel me to look upon your gold as
a bribe to draw me away from Jesus, and to
bring me back to the yoke and heavy burden
of former years, a burden which neither our
fathers nor we were able to endure. But, my
dear brother," and tears gushed from her eyes
and dripped down her long lashes as she re-

peated the tender word, " I have found purer
gold than you possess, it is 'the gold tried in
the fire,' and I am heir of a finer mansion than
you have purchased, even a mansion in heaven,
while the blessings I receive are vastly better
than annuities, for every moment they perfectly
satisfy my wants and longings, filling my heart
with a joy which no language can express. And
all this comes from my being the willing bride
of Him to whom are all things, and who is to me
a Friend that sticketh closer than a brother.
I trust that you will see that my course is the
result of deep conviction, and also of an inward
experience which daily grows more bright and
satisfactory. Henceforth my song shall be:—

> " 'Jesus, I my cross have taken,
>   All to leave and follow thee ;
> Naked, poor, despised, forsaken,
>   Thou, from hence, my all shalt be.
> Perish every fond ambition—
>   All I've sought, or hoped, or known:
> Yet how rich is my condition—
>   God and heaven are still my own!'"

This unexpected gush of eloquence, and
touching exhibition of pure devotion to Christ,
fell upon the captain like a storm upon an un-
ballasted vessel, and tears, unbidden, trickled
down his sun-tanned cheeks. Recovering himself from the first and almost overpowering

shock, he stepped forward, caught Nora in his brawny arms, and embraced her with the tenderness of a child. Human love, purified and intensified by Divine love, had conquered him. While thus caressing her, he told her that, instigated and urged by their parents and the parish priest, he had come to spirit her away, if she could be induced to enter his carriage. He then humbly begged her to forgive him for having lent himself as the mean tool of what he now saw was wicked, Jesuitical trickery—yes, he even used this word—and again embracing her, he said, "Nora, don't forget to pray for your oldest, and probably your wickedest brother!" So saying, he took his hat, and with a doubtful, hesitating step entered his carriage and moved away. From the piazza Nora watched the receding vehicle until it disappeared in the distant crowds, and then retired to her room, doubtless to pray. The next day she received a note from her brother containing some very encouraging words, and enclosing a check of a thousand dollars. She said she regarded both the words and the money as blessings directly from the Lord, but that the penitent and hopeful words of her brother gave her the greater joy.

A portion of our next interview was consumed in discussing Nora's recent experience. As a kind Providence had ordered, our whole company was present, with the addition of a young lay-preacher, by the name of Theodore, who was here to assist me in extra meetings. Consequently my study was quite as full of persons as were our hearts of interest. When, at last, the mind of the party turned to my own narrative, I began as follows:—

"On the evening of Sunday, January 15, 1854, having carefully surveyed the grounds of my individual responsibility to God, and prayerfully resolved to do my duty, I was induced for the first time to join in prayer and exhortation among Protestants. I came forward from the congregation to the altar, or anxious seat, seeking the Lord. This I did without solicitation from any one, and—my mind having been previously made up—as a hungry man comes to a savoury meal. This was one of the greatest events of my life, an important step which I have never regretted. However, I have learned that salvation is not dependent upon any outward performance, though the act be the result of an inner conviction of duty. But this step indentified me as on the side of the Lord, as one not ashamed of Him before men."

"Were you converted that night?" inquired Johnnie.

"I am sorry to say I was not. I was not yet sufficiently humbled, and, O! how ignorant of

simple, saving faith, and of the way to secure it!
One evening a brother asked me to bear my cross
in the meeting, and I was foolish enough to
think he meant that I should carry an actual
cross of wood or bone!

"And there was a prejudice in my heart
against all Protestants, and especially against
Methodists, which had grown up and strengthened with my years, besides a subtle pride of
opinion, which it was difficult to give up. I
found it was one thing to confess the follies
with the lips, and quite another to eradicate
them from the heart. When this barrier to my
progress was overcome, another presented itself
in my way. For now the question arose, as if
proposed by the Master, whether I was willing
to endure for his sake the persecution which I
knew would come upon me. I was fully aware
of the feeling of contempt which my old Roman
Catholic friends would entertain toward me.
My former experience, hard master that it was,
told me all about it. Like the Apostle Paul, I
expected the hatred and scoffs of my former
friends, their abuse, and, perhaps, physical
violence. How 'the fear of man which bringeth
a snare' bound me! For some time I struggled
like a captive with his chain. And yet, who
has not felt this galling fetter? To secure by
industry and good behaviour an unsullied repu-

tation among my fellows had been something more than a dream of my life. Now to have my name cast out as evil, to be regarded as a turncoat, an apostate, a traitor, a vagabond, to be the butt of ridicule, and the object of religious anathemas from those whose friendship I had so fully enjoyed (O! who can bear the scorn of friends!)—all this was terribly trying to my unrenewed nature. But as I was thus counting the cost, I was enabled to submit by recalling the words of Jesus: 'If any man will come after me, let him deny himself, and take up his cross daily, and follow me.' And like my Saviour, 'who made himself of no reputation, and took upon him the form of a servant,' that he might bear the sins and reproaches of us all, I saw that I must be willing to endure the offence of the cross, and be as the filth and offscouring of the world, for the Lord's sake."

"How long," questioned Monsieur Grenier, "did it take you to reach this conclusion?"

"As nearly as I can remember, it was several days. Every step I took in advance was closely contested. When one mountain peak was reached, I saw before me a still higher one to be scaled. It was like Alps on Alps piled up to heaven. Now came the question of separation from all my former friends, my brothers and sisters, and my dear mother! This seemed more than I could bear."

"O!" exclaimed Luella, "how different was your lot from mine; for when I came to Jesus, I came also to my friends who were already Christians. And yet in my heart I had to give up all; but God gave all back to me—minus my sins—with love, light, and heaven besides."

"I was soon led to see," I continued, "that if a man love father, mother, etc., more than Christ, he is not worthy of him, and that hence I must be willing to sever the dearest earthly ties, and welcome, if need be, the estate of him whose enemies are they of his own household. But my spirit struggled most and longest when I contemplated the effect of my course upon my mother, who would consider this a burning disgrace to the family name, and a stigma upon the Church of my fathers. In her view it was the greatest crime which her son could possibly commit! Her grief would be greater than could be caused by any calamity that might befall me, even death at the hands of an assassin, or on the gallows for capital crime; for to her I was to be as one hopelessly ruined for time and eternity! For weeks I hesitated at this point, unwilling to tender so bitter a cup to her lips. But at length the sorrows of Christ for me, rather than those of my friends, conquered me, and I yielded to the voice of God. Like Bunyan's Pilgrim, I put as it were, my fingers in my ears that the clamours of the world might cease to affect me, and ran on crying 'Life! life! eternal life!'"

"And was not this all the sacrifice God required at your hands?" asked Johnnie.

"Not exactly. There still remained the consecration of myself. Self, after all, is the dearest idol we worship—the greatest enemy to be overcome. Alexander the Great is said to have conquered the world, and to have wept that he could extend his conquests no farther; but self conquered and ruined him. How truly wise is the proverb, that 'He that ruleth his spirit is better than he that taketh a city.' Like the Indian who is represented as having given up for God first his blanket, then his gun, afterward his dog, and last of all himself, so I had sacrificed all things, except my will, to the control of Jesus. At length I was enabled to make an unconditional and complete surrender to him as my King, and to count all things, including my poor self, 'but loss for the excellency of the knowledge of Christ Jesus my Lord.' On the evening of March 19, 1854—memorable epoch in my history!—after two long months of fearful spiritual struggles, while

pleading vocally in prayer-meeting for the
Divine blessing, I was enabled to reach the
sublime height of the poet when he sings—

> " ' But drops of grief can ne'er repay
>   The debt of love I owe :
>   Here, Lord, 1 give myself away,—
>   'Tis all that I can do.'

" Then as I waited, by saving faith in the
promise of my Redeemer, the pure light of God
fell from the opening heaven above me, and in
my spirit I heard the sweet voice of Jesus say,
'Peace, be still.' The storm ceased, and there
was a great calm ! 'Hallelujah to God and to
the Lamb !' was the response of my ransomed
soul, and the song has grown sweeter and
sweeter until this day. I am sure it will be
more glorious still in heaven ! I then praised
the Lord aloud, and called on every one present
to praise him. The language of the psalmist
was mine : 'Let everything that hath breath
praise the Lord.' What I received was infinitely
above what I had asked or thought, and I
exulted in conscious and free salvation. I
then knew for myself, and not for another, that
Jesus' blood had washed away my sins. And,
O ! with what tender yearnings did my heart
turn toward my dear mother and all my friends,

that they too might share with me these hallowed joys, these richest gifts of heaven."

"O! pray tell us," anxiously inquired Nora, "how your mother received the news of your conversion, and what effect it had upon her and your friends.".

"But, Nora, the story is nearly as long as it is thrilling. I have already related much more than I contemplated when, on that beautiful Sabbath, Luella asked me the question which has proved to be the source of many of our joys. But as the Sabbaths will be too much occupied with public meetings to the end of this Conference year to permit us to meet of an afternoon, as we have been wont to do, should I ever give you the information you desire, and which I am very willing to impart, it must be at some future time. For the present, as a test for the blessings we have received from above, and as the means of their growth and enlargement, let us go forth to live and labour for Jesus."

As I uttered these words the Professor arose, and, in a tender mood which drew tears from all eyes, proceeded to pronounce a brief valedictory, or farewell speech, which he had evidently prepared with much care for the occasion, after which he presented to each one of us an appropriate *souvenir*, as a memorial of our profitable gatherings here. Then turning unexpectedly to

Monsieur Grenier and Nora, he gave them each a beautiful copy of the Holy Bible, accompanying the gifts with eloquent remarks, which greatly increased our reverence, and deepened our love for the Divine word. To this Monsieur Grenier attempted to respond; but entangled somewhat in bad English, as he generally is when embarrassed, and choking with emotions of gratitude, he made short but cordial work of it, and our interview terminated with his beautifully-pronounced and not easily forgotten *"Au revoir."*

NOTE.—Should the patronage given to this Canadian edition prove as good as that given to the American editions, Mr. Beaudry proposes soon to furnish for publication a sequel, containing an account of the conversion of his mother and relatives; also the thrilling facts connected with his present Mission work in Montreal.

TORONTO;

PRINTED AT THE GUARDIAN OFFICE, 78 & 80 KING ST. EAST.